"Filled with grace, deep compassion, and the necessary consolation of the natural world, John Price's *Daddy Long Legs* is a wise and articulate portrait of family and fatherhood. If this book had wings, it would settle gently onto your chest, just above the heart."   —Dinty W. Moore, author of *The Mindful Writer*

"John Price has long been the funniest man in the nature business. Now he's gotten personal and invited us into the fascinating ecosystem that is his family, a world of bugs and woodchucks, children and parents. With his characteristic wit, and a little wisdom, too, he weaves family and nature into a beautiful and inspiring story of growth."

—David Gessner, author of *Return of the Osprey*

"In the 'no-kill zone' surrounding John Price's house and yard, his kids attach freely and fiercely to bugs, tadpoles, and guy dolls. What he and his wife are really creating is a no-kill zone for the heart. Read this funny, wrenching testimony on the doubts, humiliations, and joys of committed fatherhood as you would any fine literature. But read it also as a manual on how to unearth, then build upon, your own foundations in family and place."

—Julene Bair, author of
One Degree West: Reflections of a Plainsdaughter

"When Dante wandered lost in a dark wood midway through the journey of life, he was led back onto the path by the poet Virgil. John Price was led out of his own dark wood by less famous guides—his rambunctious sons, his patient wife, a wise grandmother, countless wild creatures, and the Midwestern prairie. With grace and wit, he tells in these pages the story of how the love of people and land restored his sense of purpose, his courage in the face of loss, and his joy in living. It is an ancient story, made fresh."

—Scott Russell Sanders, author of
& Selected Essay

Daddy Long Legs

Daddy Long Legs

The Natural Education of a Father

John T. Price

Trumpeter • *Boston & London* • 2013

TRUMPETER BOOKS
An imprint of Shambhala Publications, Inc.
Horticultural Hall
300 Massachusetts Avenue
Boston, Massachusetts 02115
www.shambhala.com

©2013 by John T. Price

Photograph on the title page: Loess Hills, east of Mondamin, Iowa.
©Bill Whittaker at en.wikipedia (//en.wikipedia.org)

9 8 7 6 5 4 3 2 1

First Edition
Printed in the United States of America

⊗This edition is printed on acid-free paper that meets the
American National Standards Institute Z39.48 Standard.
♻This book is printed on 30% postconsumer recycled paper.
For more information please visit www.shambhala.com.

Distributed in the United States by Random House, Inc.,
and in Canada by Random House of Canada Ltd

Designed by James D. Skatges

Library of Congress Cataloging-in-Publication Data

Price, John, 1966–
Daddy long legs: the natural education of a father / John T. Price.—
1st ed.
p.   cm.
ISBN 978-1-61180-002-9 (pbk.: alk. paper) 1. Price, John, 1966–
2. Price, John, 1966—Family. 3. Fatherhood. I. Title.
CT275.P84267A3 2013
920—dc23
[B]
2012042976

For my family

We can do no great things,
only small things with great love.

—Mother Teresa

From wonder into wonder existence opens.

—Lao-Tzu

Contents

1

The First Worm

SPENCER CHARGED into the bedroom where I was resting.

"The first worm, Daddy! The first worm of spring!"

He stuck his fleshy, three-and-a-half-year-old fist in front of my face, allowing the mud to drip onto the white sheets. The short end of an earthworm, brown and moist, was attempting to wriggle through the hole between Spencer's palm and pinky finger.

"Wow," I replied, trying to sound enthusiastic, "that's a lively one."

"Don't you want to hold her, Daddy?" He opened his palm to show me the entire worm, more dirt spilling onto the sheets. It was long, but a little thin as far as Iowa earthworms go. Then again, it was only March—by July it might be as thick as my finger.

"Don't you want to see where I found her, Daddy?"

I didn't respond right away, and I could see the disappointment in his face. Normally, I would have put more effort into this moment. Around here, the first worm of the year is the equivalent of the first robin, the first tree buds, the first daffodil shoots. The first definitive sign that winter is nearly behind us, the season of life begun. This worm had appeared a little earlier than usual, making it even more special. Spencer's five-year-old "big" brother, Ben, would certainly make a big deal about it when he got home from preschool. At that moment, however, I wasn't very interested in worms. I was trying hard to relax and, as my doctor put it, "take a close look at my life."

Let me back up a few days.

Late in the evening, around the time of the March full moon—the Worm Moon—I was sitting at my desk, trying to write, when it felt like someone reached into my chest, grabbed my heart, and juiced it like an orange. Pain shot through my entire upper body, even my teeth. My first thought was: *Could this be the gas station burritos I scarfed for dinner?* Then it suddenly got worse, doubling me over in the chair, robbing me of breath. I thought I was going to pass out. Gradually, the pain diminished and I began to breathe normally.

Definitely the burritos, I rationalized. *Now let's get back to work.*

"*Not* the burritos," Steph insisted a couple of days later—this morning, in fact—when I first told her about the incident. You eat enough of those over a lifetime and they will kill you, but not that quickly. This was something else, she said, something serious, and she was angry I'd waited so long to tell her. She demanded I immediately see the doctor.

"That's ridiculous," I said.

"Then I'm calling an ambulance to carry you there. Lights, sirens, the whole shebang—you want that?"

An hour later, I was sitting in the doctor's office while he listened to my chest through a cold stethoscope. Dr. Tibbets was in his forties, with young children. His relative youth was one reason I'd chosen him for my doctor when we first moved to Council Bluffs eight years prior. The other was that he seemed like a fairly laid-back person, not the kind to overreact and schedule unnecessary, expensive tests.

"I don't hear anything suspicious, but we need to run some tests. First, an EKG, then a stress test to check for damage. You may have suffered some kind of stress-related cardiac event, but it could be tough to determine now. You should have come in earlier."

"Do we *really* have to do all that?" I whined. "I mean, come on, I ate a couple of bad burritos. And I'm not that stressed out—I'm not even teaching right now."

"Actually, it can be very stressful for some men to get away from their normal work schedule, especially workaholic types. How many hours do you typically work a week?"

"I don't know," I replied, truthfully. My workweek didn't really have an official beginning or end. Normally, when I wasn't teaching or preparing to teach my college courses (during the day) or writing (during the night), I was thinking about teaching and/or writing. The work schedule hadn't changed while on sabbatical that spring semester of 2006, only the nature of the work—sitting at my desk anywhere from ten to twelve hours a day, researching and writing or, as was increasingly the case, failing to write. The pressure had only increased as I tried to make up for squandered time. *Squandered* was one of my favorite words back then—squandered time, squandered talent, squandered youth. Steph said I should have it printed on the backs of all my dress shirts.

"Well, the fact that you don't know should tell you something," Tibbets continued. "As I was saying, when certain men step away from their normal work routine, auxiliary pressures can sometimes crash through the barriers and overwhelm. That might also explain why you felt compelled to eat those burritos. Have you been eating a lot of junk food recently?"

I had, actually. The reasons for this, I thought, had more to do with the family budget and my late-night work habits than any uncontrollable craving for gas-station burritos—was such a craving possible? Regardless, I decided not to share this or any other incriminating information with Tibbets. I didn't really need to.

"Trouble sleeping?"

Silence.

"Inexplicable muscle aches and pains?"

Silence.

"Bouts with depression, listlessness, irritability?"

Silence.

"OK then, shall we get on with the tests?"

When I pulled into our driveway after seeing the doctor, Spencer was crouched near the front retaining wall, turning over rocks in his Superman pajamas and red rubber boots. As usual, he was underdressed for the weather, which still carried a wintry sting. No matter what we dressed him in, he'd inevitably strip down to the minimum tolerable. This was thanks, in part, to a revolutionary potty training method we'd employed that encouraged parents to let their children run around naked until they became conscious of the need to use the toilet. They called it the "$75 Method," because that's about how much it cost to clean the carpet after the child inevitably had an accident on it. Spencer did indeed become conscious of the need to use the toilet, but apparently forgot about the need to wear clothes. In the summer, he spent much of his time completely naked—a habit we hoped to break before the teen years. I thought about asking him to put his coat back on, but he didn't seem bothered by the weather or anything else. Like most parents, we did the worrying for him, gratis.

We'd worried, for instance, that when his brother, Ben, returned to preschool after winter break, Spencer might not know what to do with himself. Those fears proved unfounded. He missed Ben, and often said so, but he never let those feelings interfere with the day's agenda. During really cold weather, he'd spend hours indoors assembling LEGO castles or making flower-shaped window decorations or taping together small household items such as pens, night-lights, loose change, tampons—anything within reach—to create esoteric sculptures resembling those in the Museum of Modern Art. He'd gone through so much Scotch tape, we'd been forced to lock it up with the drain cleaner.

Spencer also enjoyed drawing pictures for his graphic nonfiction book series, the latest of which was entitled *Tony Johnson's Bug and Creature Book*. "Tony Johnson" was a pseudonym Spencer had invented for himself when he was barely two. Where the name came from or why was a mystery, but he had since commanded it to be written on the cover pages of all his published works: *Attack of the Possums!* by Tony Johnson. *Bowling Ball Birthday Party!* by Tony Johnson. *Why I Am Amazing!* by Tony Johnson. Clearly, Tony was a far more prolific writer than I was, and his titles reflected a dramatic engagement with the world that I envied.

Whenever the weather became the least bit tolerable, however, Spencer dumped Tony Johnson, along with the art projects and the LEGOs and the clothes, and headed outdoors.

"I'm looking for worms," Spencer told me as I walked toward the front door. "Wanna help?"

"Not right now, buddy," I said. "Maybe later."

I entered the kitchen, where Steph was waiting. I told her the EKG had been normal, emphasizing again that "the event," as Tibbets called it, had probably been nothing. He was going to run me through a stress test in a few days, I told her, but that just seemed like an unnecessary and expensive formality.

"Did he prescribe any medication?"

"Just baby aspirin and some predictable advice about eating healthier and exercising." His actual advice, which I didn't share, was "You need to eat healthier, exercise, and take a close look at your life. If you want to live, that is."

I think Steph knew I wasn't telling her everything.

"Whatever this turns out to be," she said, "it's a serious wake-up call. Why don't you go upstairs and rest for a while."

Lying in bed, I thought about Tibbets's ultimatum: *If you want to live.* Of course I wanted to live—I was thirty-nine years old! My paternal grandfather, Roy, had died of a massive coronary at age sixty-nine, enjoying thirty more years of eating French dip sandwiches, collecting decorative whiskey bottles, and bonding with his grandchildren. I deserved the same, didn't I?

Despite all the warning signs my body had been sending during the last year, the idea that, at my age, I could have suffered a heart attack or might be experiencing a dangerous case of stress seemed ridiculous. As did my doctor's response. *Take a close look at my life?* What kind of prescription was that? That's what I did all the time—I was a writer whose main subject, until recently, had been his own life. And why not? I'd enjoyed a relatively privileged existence. In graduate school, while some of my classmates drafted memoirs about drug addiction and abuse and extreme family dysfunction, I was writing personal essays about growing up in Fort Dodge, Iowa, in a close-knit, loving family.

Now I was married to a woman I loved and who loved me, with two children I loved, living just a few hours from my extended family, whom I also loved. We were able to travel fairly regularly to my hometown of Fort Dodge to visit my parents and my ninety-two-year-old maternal grandmother, Kathryn, or as my boys affectionately called her, "Gramma K." I had a teaching job at a small university in Omaha, Nebraska, just across the Missouri River, and had published a well-reviewed book of nature writing. Our financial solvency was month to month, sometimes day to day—which I worried about a lot—but I was (so far) making just enough for Steph to stay home and dedicate herself full-time to raising our children. The boys were creative and smart and, I assumed, happy. Viewed from the outside, all was good.

So why wasn't it good enough?

It was a question Steph had asked me many times, usually during one of our increasingly frequent "quality-of-life" discussions. These epic confabs were normally sparked by some snarky, passive-aggressive comment from me about money. I knew when Steph quit her full-time teaching job after Ben was born that our budget would be tight, but I had no idea how tight. I'd assumed that between my teaching job and yet-to-be written books, we would be more than comfortable. That's how I'd always imagined middle age in the middle class—comfortable. Five years and one book later, we could barely afford to go out to eat at Long John

Silver's once in a while or keep the boys in shoes and underwear, most of which disintegrated into pollen dust after a couple weeks of hard use. We could probably survive without chicken planks and Underoos (especially Spencer), but then there were the mortgage payments and utilities and other necessities. There was also our drafty, century-old house—my bitter nemesis—which seemed in constant need of expensive repairs I didn't have the know-how to conquer myself. As a result of all this, we'd increasingly become dependent on the generosity of family and friends, who gave us everything from hand-me-down clothes to discarded furniture to old power tools to the occasional slab of meat.

I'd long been a critic of the male provider myth that plagued past generations of men. Now that the responsibility had fallen onto my meager shoulders, it was proving more difficult to shake off.

Steph, in contrast, was relatively content with our situation. She often recalled that when she was young her father had been temporarily laid off from his academic job, and her family—all *six* of them—had resorted to picking apples in the Idaho orchards and sleeping on picnic benches instead of hotels when traveling. This did not console me. I'd grown up in one of those comfortable middle-class families that admired crop fields from a distance, and had an air-conditioned room waiting at the end of every long-distance summer journey. We'd even had Cablevision—a luxury that now seemed miles out of reach. My family, like most, had experienced some financial difficulties, but the only personal hardship I recalled was being required to get a paper route to cover my sixth grade allowance. After a year, I was allowed to resign and get back on the parental dole.

So I considered our current situation not just a big step backward in my family's march toward economic security, but also a broken promise—hadn't we all been led to believe that, in America, each generation was supposed to be better off than the last one? Not Steph, apparently. She considered our struggles a grand and honorable adventure. She saw the decision to forego material comforts for the sake of nurturing our children as a virtuous, countercultural choice, much like Thoreau's. She was always bringing up Thoreau during these quality-of-life talks.

"Except Henry David didn't have four mouths to feed and a mortgage!" I'd countered.

Steph questioned (sometimes loudly) why I seemed incapable of appreciating all the good things we had, together, as a family. A house with a roof that only occasionally leaked. A working toilet. Each other. It wasn't healthy, she said, to be always concentrating on what's missing in life, rather than on what's already there.

I accused her, in turn, of watching too many episodes of *The Waltons*.

But she was right—it wasn't healthy. That much was apparent, as I lay in bed after my visit to the hospital. As much as I hated to admit it, Tibbets had been dead-on with the symptoms: the sleeplessness, the irritability, the bouts with depression, and on and on. During the more difficult stretches, Steph had done her best to pull me out of the ditch, including sharing more rousing stories from her picnic bench years, but there was little she could do on her own while also being attentive to the needs of our kids. I suppose Ben and Spencer couldn't help but notice my low moods as well, and also my propensity to flee to the bedroom or the writing desk whenever a family excursion was suggested. The invitations to join those excursions had become less and less frequent, and by that winter it seemed our children had finally come to accept their father's absence from the zoo trips, the walks in the nearby woods, the sledding and skating parties, the bedtime stories—his absence from the primary narrative of their family's life. Now that spring was approaching, they might leave him behind altogether.

And that could be another kind of death.

These were the symptoms, I knew, but what about the causes? It was a question that had, against my will, taken on new urgency since my visit to the hospital. Despite all my complaining about the house and the money, I instinctively understood that what I was experiencing couldn't be cured by Steph getting a job or by moving to a better domicile or by getting a 200 percent raise, though I wouldn't turn it down. The source was deeper than that, and would likely take more than an afternoon to uncover.

Stretched out on the bed, eyes closed, I had just begun to scratch at the surface when Spencer made his entrance with the worm.

"Open your hand, Daddy."

He dumped the creature into my palm along with a pile of dirt. The worm wriggled and twisted, trying to dig its way into the muddy flesh it confused for home.

"Her name is Wilma. Please come see where I found her, Daddy. *Please.*"

"OK," I said, and arose from my soil-splattered shroud.

Outside, Spencer took my hand. We walked past the retaining wall near the house where I'd seen him searching earlier, past the scraggly pear trees and the giant blue spruce, and across the open ground. The yard, like the worm, was not pretty during that time of year. A raggedy half acre, our sloping, uneven property looked naked in early spring, the veneer of snow having just retreated, exposing brown patches of grass and cold mud. Everything was mashed down and dead-looking. Sticky, baklava-like layers of leaves had accumulated against the backyard fence and in various spots where they'd blown and settled last fall. I stepped in one of the gooey piles and got a whiff of decay.

"Hurry up, Daddy!" Spencer commanded, pulling at my arm.

We passed "Neighbor Henry's" fence, peering over to see if the woodchuck had awakened from her hibernation. If she had, it's likely one of her first excursions would be to Henry's vegetable garden, digging up whatever spoils remained from last season. Henry had electrical wires running all over, which had once caused our cat Dorothy to perform a twisting half gainer in midair. She now steered clear of the place, but that was not the case with the woodchuck. Despite our affection for Henry (who was pushing eighty) and for the fresh veggies he shared with us every summer, we'd done little to help him in his battle with this animal. The woodchuck's den entrance, which we'd kept secret, was cleverly hidden inside a rubber tire Henry used to shore up the hillside along his earth home. Henry, like his adversary, lived underground, which Spencer thought should've made them friends. Last spring, we'd watched the woodchuck standing on the edge of that tire, nursing her young—two furry cherubs—and gazing out over the small, wooded valley below.

Spencer and I stepped down to the crumbling retaining wall at the far northeast corner of our property, near the woods. With the leaves gone, I could just see Cedar Lawn cemetery on the other side of the trees, its gray and white stones dotting the hillside. This part of the yard was largely uncharted territory for Spencer, and had always been a little scary with the cemetery and all, but he was clearly in the process of exploring it up close. I felt proud of his daring.

"This is where I found her," Spencer said, pointing to an overturned rock at the base of the wall. "I'm going to let her go now, so she can see her momma. Her heart's wrinkled because she misses her so much."

Always the momma, I thought.

"And you can't tell anybody where she lives, OK, because of the fishers."

Spencer was referring, yet again, to the traumatic fishing he'd experienced with some friends of ours last fall. When he first joined them on their boat, Spencer was excited to catch and release a few fish, which he'd done many times with his mother. Steph, however, had always used fake lures or, in a pinch, mashed-up wads of Wonder Bread. These people had a Styrofoam container full of live earthworms, which they proceeded to skewer on the ends of hooks. According to Ben, who'd witnessed the incident, Spencer started screaming and crying and jumping up and down in the boat. He had to be taken back to shore like one of those airline passengers who go berserk, forcing the plane to land so he can be safely removed in handcuffs.

"They kill worms!" Spencer sobbed when Steph picked him

up at the dock, jabbing his pointer finger at our friends. "They kill worms!"

Spencer's meltdown had been disconcerting. Not that I didn't like worms. I'd turned over many a rock as a child looking for them, especially the giant "night crawlers" that emerged, like vampires, after sundown. Even earlier, my favorite character in the Richard Scarry picture books had always been the worm with the little red hat—"Some animals wiggle and crawl and spell words," the caption read. Back then, after a rain shower, worms surfaced in droves in our yard and on sidewalks and driveways, escaping subterranean floods. Now, walking along residential sidewalks after a downpour, the lawns thick with chemically treated grass, I saw far fewer of them. Which was too bad, since they helped aerate the soil and add to its organic richness. Protecting worms and other earth-digging creatures, such as our children, was just one of the reasons we'd never used lawn fertilizers or herbicides. A fact that, given the weedy condition of our yard, was abundantly clear to the neighbors.

But worms are no woodchucks. No cute chirps and whistles, no Buddha belly, no cherublike offspring. And like other species we're familiar with, too many of them can cause ecological imbalance. Worms can and, in some cases, should be sacrificed as food. Robins eat them, of course, and moles and fish and a lot of other wild creatures Spencer admired. Some scientists claim that if eaten by humans, they could reduce cholesterol—a step I might be forced to take, who knew?

I'd tried to explain some of this to Spencer when he returned home from the fishing trip, but the tears continued to flow, along with the righteous indignation.

"A robin didn't kill those worms, Daddy! Mr. French did, and that's against the law!"

I glared at Steph, who just shrugged. As she well knew, Spencer was referring to a "law" created somewhere in the mist-enshrouded past that designated our house and yard and everything it contained to be part of a "No-Kill Zone." Within its borders, no one was allowed to knowingly harm or kill any living creature. I suspected the boys and their mother had created this law, but according to them it had no official beginning. It had always been and always would be, like God. This was admirable thinking, and easy to enforce with dew-eyed creatures such as woodchuck babies and speckled fawns, but it presented major challenges when applied to other species. Flies, for instance. Do we simply let them buzz around the house, and our heads, spreading germs and despair? The same puzzle presented itself when confronting a number of other household pests: mice, carpenter ants, spiders, and the occasional wasp floating through one of the torn window screens I hadn't gotten around to repairing.

There was also the problem of the boys traveling outside the boundaries of our yard, among savages and civilizations not under our legal jurisdiction. Spencer's behavior on the fishing boat suggested just one of the potential consequences. I worried that if such displays became a regular occurrence, our already endangered social circle might face total extinction.

Then again, that was just my opinion. The flies and carpenter ants and earthworms might have seen it differently.

"OK," I assured Spencer, "I won't tell anyone where the worm lives."

"Her name is *Wilma*, Daddy."

He crouched down to search for her original hole, but couldn't find it. After digging his finger into the dirt to start a new one, he tried to coax her into it, but she just squirmed around on the surface. Apparently, that spot of dirt wasn't good enough for her anymore. She wanted something better. *Just who does she think she is?* I thought. More than a worm? A metaphor? A squiggly sign of subterranean imbalance? Of mortality—*The worms crawl in, the worms crawl out, the worms play pinochle on my snout?* I looked again at the cemetery on the other side of the trees, and wondered: If I'm buried there, perhaps sooner than expected, will Wilma's offspring find me and recognize one of their own? A fellow creature who'd once wiggled and crawled and spelled words?

Spencer gave up looking for Wilma's original hole and turned over another rock. There was an unexpected scattering of roly-polies and a small centipede, as well as the glistening strata of another half-submerged earthworm. Their appearance in our yard, like Wilma's, was earlier than usual. I immediately thought of global warming, but not Spencer. His eyes widened—the cold earth appeared to be giving birth—and he started touching the bugs with his fingers, chasing the centipede into the brown grass and scaring the roly-polies into becoming little balls he could roll around like marbles. Talk about stress.

It seemed like a good time for me to escape—I had some serious thinking to do, after all. I quietly made my way to the kitchen door, but before going inside, I took another look back at Spencer. He hadn't noticed my absence. He was in the process of turning over yet another rock, then jumping aside to avoid crushing his toes. He crouched down close to the earth, his red boots standing out starkly against the bland winter colors. I couldn't tell what new life he was discovering there. Only that I was missing it.

2

Not So Golden Nuggets

HERE'S SOMETHING I can tell you: there comes a time in a man's life when he doesn't want to open the door to his car and find a pile of mouse turds in the driver's seat.

That's exactly what happened as I was getting ready to drive to the office. It had been a couple of weeks since I'd visited campus, and I was actually looking forward to it. I'd even dressed up a bit—Oxford shirt, chinos, the shiny brown shoes, and (of course) the tweed jacket my father had given me when I became a professor. I thought I might just breeze into the English department, chat with colleagues, file a few things stacked on my office floor, change the postcards on the door. Some real work. Given how the writing was progressing, I could have used a sense of accomplishment, cheaply purchased.

I needed a distraction from the health worries as well. The day before, during the cardiac stress test at the hospital, they'd run me hard on an inclined treadmill—like a laboratory mouse, actually—until my heart rate reached a certain level just this side of vomiting. Then they'd pumped my heart full of radioactive solution and put me in a dark room to take some images. While under a large, slow-moving machine called a "gamma camera," I found myself flashing back to the opening of my favorite television show as a boy, *The Incredible Hulk*, only with me in the starring role: *Dr. John Price, professor, writer, searching for a way to tap into the hidden strengths that all humans have. Then an accidental overdose of gamma radiation interacts with his unique body chemistry. And now as Dr. Price grows angry or outraged, or just annoyed, a startling metamorphosis occurs.* . . . At some point during that procedure, I'd peeked over the shoulder of the technician and seen my heart lit up in florescent yellow, red, blue, and, yes, *green*. No one at the hospital had given me a hint of what it all meant, and I was still waiting, trying to be optimistic. Going to my office was part of that effort.

But that's how it goes, doesn't it? You dress up a little, you're headed to the office, you're feeling momentarily healthy and accomplished and professional . . . and then a goddamned mouse craps all over your car.

Funny how the small things matter.

I called the whole trip off and stormed back into the house to get something to clean up the mess. What's the best thing for cleaning mouse turds off car seats? I had no idea, and there was no one around to ask—Stephanie was out running errands with Ben and Spencer. I figured paper towels would smear the stuff deeper into the fabric, and getting it wet would be even worse. I could have tried lifting our ancient, smoke-spewing vacuum down to the car, but that machine was too busy auditioning for the next *Terminator* movie. Perhaps an old-fashioned brush and dustpan? If I kept the car door open while sweeping, I might avoid inhaling fecal dust and contracting hantavirus—or was that just a danger with aged fecal dust? That might be the kind of information I could find on the Internet, but first I needed to locate the dustpan, which was no small task. I had just started digging through the junk pile in our kitchen closet, discovering yet more evidence of mouse activity, when Steph walked in.

"What are you doing in there?"

"A goddamned mouse got in my car and crapped all over my seat. Now I have to clean it up."

"Oh."

I sensed a story coming on.

"About that . . . um . . . you see, the boys and I were transferring a couple of mice we found in the live trap, and, well, um, they accidentally got loose in your car."

"What?"

"We searched all over, but we couldn't find them. We left one of the car doors open a crack last night, hoping they'd escape."

"*What?*"

"Calm down or you'll have another heart attack."

"Is that your diagnosis? A heart attack?"

"Until we hear different, *yes*. And in case you're wondering, the names of the mice are Mike and Marsha. I'm sure they'll leave on their own, sooner or later."

Again with the names. "Mike and Marsha" were just the latest in a long line of mice we'd caught in our live trap that season. Because of legal complexities within the No-Kill Zone, we couldn't use snap-traps or poison like normal people. There was a time when I wouldn't have even considered it. Mice had starred in a number of my favorite books as a kid—*Stuart Little, Mrs. Frisby and the Rats of NIMH*—not to mention the Mickey Mouse and "Tom and Jerry" cartoons. I'd even owned a pet mouse in college, Ernest T. Bass, named for the lovesick hillbilly on *The Andy Griffith Show*. Pets had been strictly forbidden at the rental house where I lived at the time, but I didn't care. I trained Ernest to run up and down my arms and perch on my shoulder while I read a book or was working on a term paper. In turn, he nurtured in me a greater appreciation for the affectionate, intelligent nature of the common rodent.

Then I bought a house of my own, the same drafty old thing

we currently occupied. During our first winter here, in 1998, we didn't use traps at all. We had other worries. Despite our new teaching jobs, the down payment on the house and some unexpected repairs had left us completely broke—I mean, not one penny in the bank and escalating credit card balances. I wondered how or if we could ever recover. This first round with pauperdom hardened us in some ways, but when it came to small and similarly impoverished creatures, we remained sympathetic. Like poor Professor Herzog in Saul Bellow's novel, eating some rodent-nibbled bread, we believed we "could share with rats, too."

But did the rodents reciprocate? Far from it. Smelling weakness, they proceeded to invade. Our cats, Dorothy and Tigger, tried to hold the frontlines, but they were no good at killing anything either. They soon returned, full-time, to eating, napping, and filling the litter box. The mice quickly had the run of the place, nibbling their way through everything from toothpaste tubes to Steph's scrapbooks to my unpublished manuscripts (no loss there) to any baked goods not locked in a steel safe. They scattered their foul nuggets everywhere—inside my shoes, under the couch, in the bookshelves, and especially in our kitchen drawers. I can't remember how many times we had to clean and disinfect our silverware, plates, and glasses. One time, Steph opened a kitchen drawer to pull out a tablecloth and a nest of squirming pink mouselings fell onto the floor. Her shrieks still haunt my nightmares.

The next winter, Steph and I went to a hardware store and purchased a live trap. It had a wind-up, metal flap that would swing down and spank the mice into a secure, fully ventilated chamber to await relocation. It worked OK, but sometimes—too often, really—the mice would get their tiny heads stuck in the flap and, well, the results weren't pretty. Around the time Spencer was born, we finally found a spankless model that met our practical and ethical needs. We'd since caught dozens of mice without any casualties, transferring them safely to a small plastic cage where the boys were free to observe and, of course, name them. Then, usually the same day, we'd pile into the car, drive to a nearby grassy field, and have a "born free" ceremony, during which we'd all sing that awful song. We rationalized that out there in the wintry fields—as free as the wind blows (and blows and blows)—the mice at least had a fighting chance for survival.

That may have been overly optimistic, but to be frank, I was beginning not to care. The mouse rescue ritual was getting a little old. Especially during extended arctic freezes when the boys would loudly protest kicking Mickey or Stuart or Mrs. Frisby out into the cold, and we'd end up housing and feeding them for weeks.

Now two of them had escaped and soiled my beloved Toyota Tercel.

"It's just a few droppings," Steph said, as I continued to search for the dustpan. "Aren't you being kind of overprotective of that old car?"

I suppose I was, but when it came to the Tercel, I was more than a tad sentimental. It was the first car Steph and I purchased as newlyweds, in 1992, while in our mid-twenties. When we spotted it on the used car lot, we remarked on its compact size, great gas mileage, and low price. During the test drive, we were blown away by the modern amenities never before enjoyed in the hand-me-down clunkers we'd always driven: a radio/cassette player, a working air conditioner, a steering wheel that didn't automatically set off the horn when turning to the left. And it was white! My grandparents had always proclaimed white cars to be the best—the best at reflecting the sun, the best at hiding dents, the best at impressing the neighbors. I would eventually regret that whiteness, which, along with the ice-blue interior, made it feel sometimes as if I was driving around inside a breath mint or a spider's egg sac. Plus, when parked alongside a snowbank, it tended to blend into the background. More than one snowplow driver had buried it alive.

Even so, some of the most profound experiences of my life had taken place in that car. Nothing sexual, which, given the cramped interior, would have caused serious injury—though I had nearly been killed in it once. In 1993, while driving down a four-lane highway, a stray pheasant flew in the open driver's side window, flapped around in my face, and caused me to almost dump the car in a ditch. That absurd, terrifying experience made me look at the seemingly ordinary Iowa landscape with new eyes—and not for the last time that summer. Steph had just landed her first teaching job near the small town of Belle Plaine, Iowa, and we moved there during one of the worst floods in recent history. I was commuting from our apartment (in yet another old house) to the University of Iowa, an hour away, where I was finishing my doctorate. During my drives along the flooded Iowa River that summer, I observed a lot of destruction, but also a wild beauty I hadn't really appreciated while growing up in the state—shimmering cottonwood groves and colorful stretches of native grasses and flowers and thousands and thousands of birds. Since I was a teenager, I had always intended to leave the Midwest for someplace prettier, by which I meant anyplace with a mountain or forest or ocean. Now I wondered if I'd missed something important.

The next summer, again in the Tercel—another name for a male falcon—I traveled to some of the largest remaining native grasslands in the Midwest and Great Plains, camping and experiencing for the first time their grandeur and beauty. That journey inspired a desire to write about and help restore the prairies of Iowa. A desire to stay home and make a difference.

I would look back on that summer as a kind of death of an old self and a rebirth—and the Tercel as one of the midwives. Now, a dozen years and nearly 200,000 miles later, it still served as a daily reminder of that journey, that profound change, that youthful freedom. My newfound commitment to place had been one of the main reasons I'd accepted the Omaha job over another at a large university near the Rocky Mountains. The possibility of residing among the Loess Hills—an American natural treasure—made this area even more appealing. Known as the "fragile giants," these two-hundred-foot-high, bullocky hills run the entire western edge of Iowa, along the Missouri River. They were created thousands of years ago, as the last of the glaciers retreated and windblown silt began piling up along the river's ancient shore. Beneath the trees and grass, they still resemble giant sand dunes. Their dramatic size was rivaled only by the now mostly destroyed loess hills along the Yellow River of China, which got its name from the flourlike soil (called "sugar clay" around here) coloring its waters. Countless people once passed by those hills along the ancient Silk Road, which, among other things, first brought paper and gunpowder to the West.

In America, native tribes considered the Loess Hills sacred, and the Ioway believed them to be the location of a "Sun Bridge" from which the dead departed for the afterlife. Lewis and Clark viewed the Loess Hills with awe during their journey up the Missouri River in 1804, and had their first official meeting with Native Americans near here—an event memorialized by the name of our town, Council Bluffs. Back then, explorers witnessed a prairie country teeming with wildlife: grizzly and wolves and bison and cougars, as well as countless birds and insects and fish. One of the members of the Lewis and Clark expedition, Sergeant Charles Floyd, wrote in his journal that this country of hills and prairie was "the Butifules . . . I ever saw." Then he promptly died from a ruptured appendix.

Iowa has since become the most ecologically decimated state in the union, with less than one-tenth of 1 percent of its native habitats remaining. The majority of what's left of Iowa prairie is found in the Loess Hills, though you couldn't tell from looking at our yard, which is set atop one of those hills and is dominated by large trees and flowering shrubs. The hills are still home to a number of rare insects, birds, and reptiles with cool names like spadefoot toad and Great Plains skink and regal fritillary butterfly—even an endangered creature called the plains pocket mouse. Nonetheless, entire hills and everything they sustain continue to be destroyed for landfill and new development. Back then, it seemed I couldn't drive anywhere in town or the surrounding area without seeing one of those ancient giants being sliced in half, like bread, or cratered or removed altogether, leaving nothing behind, not even memory.

"The Fatal Frontier," I sometimes called it.

This was yet another imperfect situation for which I felt responsible. As a self-proclaimed environmentalist, or just someone who called this place home, why wasn't I doing more to help save the Loess Hills? Was it even possible to save them? While still in grad school, inspired by my trip across the grasslands in the Tercel, I'd participated in prairie restoration and even wrote about the experience in my first book, *Not Just Any Land*. When Steph and I first settled in Council Bluffs, and for a while after Ben was born, we'd traveled to nearby prairie sites for hikes and picnics. Those visits had gradually tapered off, and now they were almost nonexistent. Part of it was my increasingly busy work schedule, but it was also depressing to witness the ongoing destruction of the hills—and why invite my children into that pain? Why encourage them to become attached to a natural place that might, perhaps overnight, end up as landfill for yet another Iowa McMansion or highway expansion or soybean processing plant?

Since moving to this area, I'd settled into a life that, although certainly close to home, seemed to be carrying me farther away every year. Instead of prairie restoration, I'd become preoccupied with home repairs and full-time teaching and earning tenure and, apparently, working my way toward an early death. Even my interests as a writer were edging away from life in this threatened environment, and toward what I'd thought (wrongly) to be the more pleasing and lucrative escape of fiction. That's what I was failing to write that sabbatical, a novel.

Inside the Tercel, however, I enjoyed a temporary reprieve from all these concerns. It remained my taxi of hope. My way back.

But how do you explain this to others? To your children, for example, whom you love beyond measure, but who have also dinged the white paint with fistfuls of gravel and side-scraped it with tricycle handlebars and colored the armrests with permanent markers and left cookie crumbs on the floor and accidentally released mice who crapped all over the driver's seat? Children who are prepared to show more mercy for a worm or a mouse than for your aging dreams?

Of course, I hadn't been easy on the Tercel myself. I'd long engaged in what my mechanic friend Andy called "delayed maintenance"—similar to the approach I took with my body—and now the expense was quickly surpassing my ability to justify it. Nonetheless, I vowed never to get rid of that car. So after finally locating the dustpan and brush, I carefully cleaned out the mouse turds—as I had the pheasant feathers and prairie dirt and cookie crumbs—and parked it in the garage.

The next morning, I still hadn't heard from the hospital, which I was sure meant bad news. I no longer felt compelled to go to the office—*Why bother if I'm going to die?*—but still wanted to get out of the house for a while. Before getting behind the wheel of the Tercel, I carefully examined the seats and floors for any sign of Mike and Marsha. I didn't spot any. As I backed into the driveway, I noticed again how the land behind our house drops off into the woods before rising into the cemetery, revealing the contours of the original loess hill. The cemetery was home to remnant groves of what some call "grandmother oaks," giant burr oaks dating back to when these hills were mostly prairie savannah. The turkey buzzards would soon return from the South American tropics to roost in their branches. A few people had complained that the buzzards gave the cemetery a morbid atmosphere and should be chased off. When I saw them, I thought instead about the old legends in which buzzards guide the souls of the dead to heaven. With or without a buzzard or a Sun Bridge, some of us were going to need all the help we could get.

It has been said that a place isn't truly home until your kin are buried there. As far as I knew, we didn't have any family buried at Cedar Lawn, but it wasn't beyond the realm of possibility. Grandma K's maternal grandmother, Josephine Hannon Porter, grew up in a large family in the nearby town of Defiance—perhaps some of them are at rest here. Regardless, Ben and Spencer represent the seventh generation in our family to live in western Iowa, which might be another way to define a place as home. The living, as well as the dying.

Speaking of dying, about a mile or so down the road from our house, the Tercel began acting strange, coughing a little, like it was having trouble breathing. Like it had hantavirus. After nearly stalling at a traffic light, it coughed and sputtered its way to the nearest mechanic.

"Take a look at this," he said to me, from behind the raised hood.

I saw that he'd removed the top from a circular something in the engine. Within the exposed cavity, there was a thick nest made of shredded cloth and patterned fragments I recognized as belonging to an old blanket in our garage.

"You had yourself a mouse living in here. I've seen it before, especially during colder months. I can't promise it's the cause of all your problems, but do you want me to clean it out?"

"Absolutely."

As I sat in the waiting room, I worried over the expensive bill to come. What would it take this time to keep my falcon on the wing? Still, it could have been worse, I thought. Imagine if the mechanic had discovered the bodies of Mike and Marsha in there, hearts frozen from fear and regret. Even worse, a squirming pink pile of mouslings. Imagine having to make that kind of life-or-death decision, alone, so far from the borders of the No-Kill Zone.

I'd like to think it would have given me pause.

3

Terror of the Triops

GRANDMA K couldn't have chosen a more inconvenient moment to tell me she was going to end her life.

On the kitchen floor, Steph and the boys were gathered around a shallow dish of water, screaming and shouting. The last two Triops were about to eat each other alive. I don't know what Santa was thinking when he left the Triops kit under the Christmas tree in December—he must have missed the warning in his magic gift catalog clearly stating these small, aquatic crustaceans "from the Age of the DINOSAURS" will cannibalize each other and traumatize children.

Steph and I had overlooked that detail as well, naively assuming that raising these creatures would be an interesting and, more important, easy science lesson for the boys—YOU CAN'T MAKE A MISTAKE! the package trumpeted. And Triops are interesting. The species dates back to the Triassic Age, and can still be found in the wild all over the world. They have very short lives, only twenty to ninety days, all of it spent swimming and breeding in temporary pools that dry up during seasonal droughts. When the water vanishes, the adult Triops die, but their embryos survive in a state of suspended animation called *diapause,* waiting for the rains to return so they can safely hatch and begin the cycle all over again. They can remain in diapause for more than twenty-five years. The website touted the scientific importance of studying this process: "Our neurophysiologist Eugene Hull, PhD, studies diapause in the hope of extracting the clock-stopping chemical found in the eggs. He believes that it could be used to suspend cellular growth in humans. Imagine the potential uses: slowing the aging process, putting a stop to cancer growth, or even easing space travel!"

We'd tried sharing some of these fascinating facts with the boys, but their interest didn't extend much beyond the advertised promise that Triops are "the pet dinosaur you can hatch yourself!" I think they half-expected to see a miniature T. rex or triceratops swimming around in the bottom of our casserole dish. Soon after carefully preparing and heating the water and sprinkling in the pepperlike eggs, the first baby Triops began squiggling around. At first they were nearly impossible to see, around fifty bright little dust motes, but as they grew, shedding their exoskeletons along the way, they came to resemble not so much dinosaurs as miniature horseshoe crabs.

This was a bit disappointing for Ben and Spencer—"No stegosaurus?!"—and their interest waned. For several weeks the casserole dish sat virtually ignored in a corner of the kitchen counter, though Steph continued to feed them as instructed. On the occasions when the boys did show an interest, the Triops did their best to be entertaining. Their feathery, frilly legs and long swallowtails propelled them through the water, where they performed endearing acrobatics—flipping, twisting, swimming upside down. Their three eyes, when observed through the magnifying glass, were "freaky" (as Ben put it). And there were other surprises. One day,

Ben noticed a strange creature swimming around in the pool, longer and skinnier than the Triops, with only two eyes on the sides of its head. We eventually identified it as a fairy shrimp, which Spencer promptly named Tinker Bell. A cute little stowaway among the "dinosaurs."

The next day Tinker Bell disappeared. What had happened to her? An extensive investigation failed to turn up any clues, not even a corpse. We noticed, however, that the population of Triops had also thinned. It had been over a month since they'd hatched, so we assumed they (and probably Tinker Bell) had simply died of old age, the normal cycle of life. Ben and Spencer became more emotionally involved with the Triops that remained, checking their status daily, and naming them according to size and/or swimming habits: Flip, Loopy, Godzilla, and so forth. The individual Triops nevertheless continued to vanish—completely. There were no floating bodies, as there had been with the deceased goldfish in the family. Not even pieces of bodies. Nothing. Steph and I could have researched this phenomenon further, but why complicate the situation with facts? The boys were sad when a particular Triops perished, but the simplicity of the process seemed to soften the blow. There was no mess. They just died and disappeared.

"Maybe they grow wings and fly to heaven," Spencer offered.

"Maybe," we responded, hoping.

Then, one afternoon, Ben and Spencer were observing Junior, the smallest remaining Triops, shed his exoskeleton, when suddenly Augustus Gloop, the largest Triops, attacked, killed, and ate him. All of him. While Ben ran to tell us the gross details, Spencer retreated to his private place behind the couch, where he began sobbing. We explained to Spencer that the attack was probably an isolated incident, that Augustus was just a big bad egg, and that maybe we only needed to give them all a bit more food. Telling him this was, despite the promise on the package, a serious mistake. After Junior's demise, the cannibalistic orgies became an almost daily occurrence. Spencer was inconsolable, no longer trusting our so-called explanations, and even Ben squirted a few tears as, one-by-one, Moby, Jiggle, and Tubesock met their horrific ends at the feathery hands of their Triassic siblings.

It didn't take three eyes to see how messed-up that was.

The morning Grandma K called, the final two Triops—Augustus Gloop and Dr. Octopus—were fighting it out to be the last of their generation. I was all for letting the situation run its course before we had to enroll the boys in therapy, but they and their mother were now noisily engaged in trying to separate the two combatants. The boys were using chopsticks to isolate them, while Steph repeatedly attempted to scoop them up with a spoon. The intent was to transfer each to a separate dish, where they (and we) could live out the final days in relative peace. But you don't survive two million years of eating your own kind only to be thwarted by a few hairless, Johnny-come-lately primates wielding twigs. The little monsters kept eluding separation and capture, taking pieces out of each other along the way. Hence, the screaming.

I was getting ready to escape to the study, as usual, when the phone rang. The digital display identified the caller as "Unknown." Normally I would have just let it ring, but I thought it might be my friend Andy calling with news about his upcoming wedding.

"John? Is that you?"

"Yes, Grandma." I couldn't hide the disappointment in my voice, seeing that it wasn't Andy, and I braced myself for another lecture about not calling more often. It had been several months since I'd been back to Fort Dodge to visit Grandma and my parents. During the previous year, I'd mostly cut myself off from friends and relatives, including the families of my younger sisters Carrie Anne and Allyson, who both lived in eastern Iowa, and Susan, who lived in Montana. It wasn't anything they'd done, or any conscious decision on my part; I'd just been too busy (or tired or sick) to return calls and e-mails. Most of them had been remarkably understanding—they were busy themselves—but not Grandma. She never missed an opportunity to remind me how seldom I called or visited her at the Friendship Haven assisted living center, where she resided in an apartment with her Chihuahua, Niña. The last we'd talked was shortly after Valentine's Day, when she called to thank the boys for sending her the two big paper hearts, which they'd colored and decorated with glitter glue and a red-and-silver avalanche of sequins. She said she'd taped them to her picture window and promised to keep them there forever.

"Sometimes the sequins fall off and sparkle in the sunlight, like the dust fairies," I overheard her telling Spencer on the phone. "It's very pretty. You could see it for yourself, if that father of yours would ever bring you."

I kept promising her I would, but like a lot of our promises to loved ones, it was easily forgotten.

"What's all that screaming?" she asked over the phone.

"Just the boys playing."

"That doesn't sound like playing to me. It sounds like murder. Is everything OK?"

"Yes," I said, as I took the phone upstairs to the study, where I shut the door. I flopped down in the recliner. "So how are you doing, Grandma?"

"Lots better," she said. "Now that I'm off this medicine."

Not again, I thought. Over the years, her doctor had made multiple changes to her prescriptions, which she took for diabetes, kidney ailments, arthritis, chronic bladder infections, and other maladies. I'd witnessed her daily, excruciating ritual of swallowing multiple pills, each followed by a small sip of juice. When one med lost its effectiveness, or caused some humiliating side effect, Grandma would lobby the doctor for a change. My mother, a registered nurse, had to carefully monitor the shifting prescriptions and their requirements in order to keep Grandma safely informed.

"Which medicine did you stop taking this time?" I asked.

"All of them."

"Excuse me?"

"John, I decided a while ago to stop taking all my meds, and I can't begin to describe the positive difference. They've made me so sick over the years I've forgotten what it feels like to be healthy.

And they've been fogging my brain, so I can't think straight. They've—"

"But you can't just quit your meds," I interrupted, suddenly annoyed at this new game she was playing. Was she after more sympathy, attention? "Those meds are keeping you alive. If you quit taking them, who knows how long you'll last?"

"The doctor says a couple of months, at best. It'll probably be a kidney infection that gets me, but I've been told they can help treat the pain."

"*What*? Grandma, this is—"

"I've had enough, honey." Her voice was gentle, but firm, as if she were addressing the child I used to be. "I'm ninety-two. How much longer do you think I have, even on the medicine? This way, I can finish my life relatively comfortable and with some dignity. I'll miss you and that wonderful family of yours—you know how much I worship you. I'll miss everyone in our family, and my friends and my little dog. That's the hardest part, leaving everyone, but as the Bible says, there's a time for everything under the sun. Besides, maybe you'll visit me more often now."

She was actually laughing.

"Have you talked this over with Mom?"

"Yes, and she's supportive, but it's hard for her. I don't know what I would've done without her these last few years. She's a saint, John, a *saint,* and I hope every one of you kids finally start realizing that. She's going to need your help. It's hard to lose your mother, I know. Someday you'll know too."

"Grandma—"

"Well, sweetie, I need to make a few more calls, so I'll let you go. Give Stephanie and the boys a hug for me when they stop screaming. Give yourself a hug too."

I sat in the chair after she hung up, considering the implications of what I'd just heard. Grandma had talked about her death before, casually tossing out lines like "I'm ready to die" or "Sometimes I feel like giving up"—but that seemed a normal by-product of growing old. Steph's grandfather Lloyd, who'd lived to be ninety-six, had done the same thing, predicting his imminent demise over a decade before it actually occurred. But this time there was something in Grandma's voice—a quiet conviction that made me uneasy.

I picked up the phone and called my mother, fully expecting her to ease my fears.

"I'm glad Grandma called you," she said. "You needed to hear it from her."

She confirmed that Grandma K had stopped taking her meds, and that she likely wouldn't make it to the end of the summer. She'd told Mom she had been seriously considering this for over a year and had thought through the consequences. Grandma insisted it was her decision, and that nothing would change her mind. Mom was going to respect that, and thought we should as well. I started to ask her more pointed questions—*Is Grandma in command of her senses? What does the doctor think? Has anyone tried to talk her out of this? Why now?*—but before we got very far, her voice broke, and she said she had to go.

"We'll talk later," she said, and hung up.

I couldn't believe what I was hearing. Although I hadn't visited my grandmother much recently, I'd taken her presence in our family as a given, the bedrock of all our relations. I knew, at her age, she probably didn't have many years left, but that inevitability had always been an abstraction, no matter how often she tried to remind us of it.

And I'd certainly never considered she would *choose* to die. I didn't know much about her life, a fact that suddenly took on new significance, but what I did know made this choice seem completely out of character. She was, if anything, a survivor. She'd survived a difficult childhood—her father's abandonment and a pair of irresponsible stepfathers; her mother, Nina's, absence while trying to support Grandma and her little sister, Virginia; the loneliness while being raised on her grandparents' farm. She'd married my fun-loving but alcoholic grandfather whom she met as a teenager in Fort Dodge, raised my mother, then followed Grandpa Andy to Green Valley, Arizona, after he retired from the Fort Dodge Gas and Electric Company. Ten months later, he suffered a paralyzing stroke and she steadfastly cared for him for nearly twenty years.

Along the way, my grandmother had survived the hardships of the Great Depression, the ravages of cancer treatment in the 1950s, a lifelong kidney ailment, the suicide of her sister, and the steady physical and mental decline of her husband. I'd been told she'd nursed several family members through terminal illnesses— her grandmother Josephine, her mother, Nina, her nephew Billy, who was just a toddler—refusing to let them die without a fight.

Now she was just giving up?

Her medical regimen was severe, no one could argue with that, and there'd been a lot of bitterness and regret in her life—a fact she'd been more than willing to share at otherwise festive family gatherings. But now she was residing in Friendship Haven with her beloved Chihuahua, surrounded by friends and regularly visited by family, including my mother, my sisters, and her seven great-grandchildren. Including me. Sure, I'd been a bit neglectful of her recently, but for what I thought were all the right reasons— the same reasons I'd neglected everyone else in the family, including my own wife and children. I was trying to be a responsible provider. Surely she'd never questioned my love for her. Surely she understood how much Ben and Spencer, who'd spent a lot of time with her while visiting my parents in Fort Dodge, worshipped and adored her.

Grandma had often told me I should feel "lucky" to have a family like mine, but didn't that cut both ways? Weren't we enough reason to get up in the morning, to keep living?

Her matter-of-fact tone didn't help. It reminded me of how my paternal grandmother, Mildred, met her end. After my grandfather Roy Price died of a heart attack in 1982 (no "choice" for him),

Grandma Mildred continued to live independently in their small apartment just a block from my parents' house in Fort Dodge. In 2002, at age ninety-three, she was diagnosed with brain cancer. She told us over the phone (again, the phone!) that she'd decided against surgery, even though it might prolong her life. She'd also apparently decided against any public displays of grief or soul-searching. Whenever any of us began to get a little weepy, she would gently cut us off. "Oh, John," she'd say, patting my hand. "These things happen. Now let's go to Village Inn for pie." She'd stunned even her longtime friends, calling them the day after her diagnosis to confirm that although there was a large tumor in her brain, they should still expect her for bridge on Thursdays.

What is wrong with these old women? I thought. *Doesn't life matter to them?*

That was a question I probably should've been asking myself on a more regular basis. Here was yet another reason my grand-mother's phone call was inconvenient. A couple of days after the cardiac stress test, Dr. Tibbets had finally called to tell me the data was inconclusive, but that nothing suggested heart damage. He said it was unlikely we'd ever know the cause of the "event," or even what it was, but I should still take it seriously. He empha-sized the need to immediately report additional symptoms, and to continue to make healthy choices, physically and emotionally.

I'd promised to follow his advice, but without the immediate threat of death, it hadn't taken long to start slipping back into old habits. This included stressing out over finances and the need to finish a manuscript before the end of sabbatical. The clock was ticking, louder than ever.

My grandmother's decision to end her life would—I think I sensed it even then—force me to continue confronting the nature and quality of my own life, just when I thought I was once again free to repress those difficult questions. My initial response to this was resentment. Sitting in my ratty recliner, I considered every-thing Grandma's decision would mean for our family, for *me*, in the coming months: the worry, the travel, the emotional mess, the time. There goes sabbatical, I thought; there goes the novel and any hope I had of singlehandedly lifting us out of our mean financial state.

Couldn't she put it off for a year?

It was then that I experienced one of those moments when it feels like your skull is turned inside out, exposing all the rottenness—a place where the death worms are already at play. One of those moments when you hardly recognize yourself as a human being.

The phone rang. The display read "Unknown"—Andy? I hesitated, then let the call go to the answering service. I got out of the chair and headed downstairs. Steph and the boys were still in the kitchen, bent over the casserole dish. There were no more screams, no frantic gestures with spoons or chopsticks. Something had been resolved, but in which direction I couldn't tell. They were completely quiet, as if meditating.

Should I interrupt them with my news? How would I tell Ben and Spencer? How would they respond? Did I really need to tell them? What were my responsibilities as a father? The boys were currently experiencing the finale of a nearly three-month performance of "Survival of the Fittest: Triassic Style," and now I was going to hit them with the fact that their beloved Grandma K was dying? And on purpose?

I was no longer resentful, I was afraid. For my sons, for my grandmother, for my mother . . . for me. If Grandma went through with her plan, where would I find the means to help my children understand it? How would it change them? How would it change all of us?

The boys didn't take any notice of me and my private worries. Their eyes were still locked on the Triops that were in the casserole dish, or used to be. Beyond them, the open window gave way to spring, to the occasional sunlit spark of an insect, the chorus of birds, the newly warm breeze in the green, budding branches. A stray gust lifted a tuft of Spencer's hair but didn't disturb his attention. I considered how whatever ending had ensued among the Triops might be given meaning by those larger, natural cycles.

Or was it the other way around, the small giving articulation and meaning to the large?

The question seemed important, but as with other complexities, I was not yet prepared to confront the challenge. I was only prepared to watch and wait and hope for the best.

Abiding, at least for the moment, in the diapause.

4

Questions with Wings

EASTER IS NOT the ideal time to talk with children about death.

That's what I was thinking in the car, heading to Fort Dodge on Holy Saturday. It had been a couple of years since we'd spent Easter with my folks, and the first chance we'd had to visit my grandmother since she'd announced her decision. I didn't know what to expect, only that I wasn't ready for it. In the intervening weeks, I'd tried to find the ideal moment to talk with the boys about how Grandma K might not be with us much longer, but such a moment never presented itself. Now we would soon be among people for whom the issue would be, I assumed, a frequent topic of discussion. My sisters and their children were spending the holiday with in-laws, so they wouldn't be there to distract the boys. Ben and Spencer would undoubtedly pick up the gist of the adult conversations and be completely confused, maybe even traumatized.

Or would they?

It was hard to predict. The power of holiday candy and toys to overcome existential despair should never be underestimated. Ben and Spencer were already counting the treasure in the backseat of the car.

"Last year I got three peanut butter eggs from the Easter Bunny and a pack of Yu-Gi-Oh! cards."

"Yeah, he gave me a giant chocolate bunny and an ant farm."

"This year, I hope he leaves me a Wonka Bar and my very own rake."

"Yeah, and another giant chocolate bunny."

"Yeah, and a real puppy."

There'd be disappointment regarding that last item—as there was every major holiday and birthday—but it was just one more reality I was unprepared to talk about at the time.

When we pulled into the drive, my parents stepped out the front door to greet us. My father was, as usual, the western gentleman in his brown Stetson hat, colorful western shirt, dark blue jeans, and custom-fitted cowboy boots with (I guessed correctly) the grass-green leather on the shank, for Easter. My mother was beside him, waving and smiling, dressed comfortably in a knit sweater and long denim skirt. They were in their late sixties and still living in the town where they graduated from high school. Dad continued his family law practice there, while Mom had recently retired after thirty years as a special education nurse.

The boys ran into their arms, while I unloaded several large suitcases Steph had stuffed to near bursting. She was not known as a light packer. As I hauled them upstairs, I recalled the day in 1974 when Mom and Mrs. Kelley took us kids on our first tour of that house. We lived one house over at the time, but when Mom became pregnant with my brother James, Dad decided we needed more room. So he bought this place from the Kelleys, right next door. I was seven, and couldn't believe our good luck. Not that I didn't like the house we lived in; I would especially miss the basement, with its rotting pile of logs in the old coal room. That's where all our fugitive hamsters inevitably turned up dead. We called it The Place Where Hamsters Go to Die. There was a playroom in the basement as well, with lopsided wall shelves loaded down with tubs of Tinkertoys and Lincoln Logs and Fisher-Price play sets representing various modern architectural triumphs—a farm, an airport, a parking ramp. In the corner was a stained, musty mattress on which my sisters and I bounced around until Susan, the youngest at the time, bounced off and broke her collarbone. The upstairs was less inspiring, except for the deep closets and the laundry chute—a kind of trapdoor into which I'd once pushed my cousin and, more than once, peed.

The Kelley place, however, was the sun around which we kids orbited. A thin, grassy acre with sixty-foot maples, spruce, walnuts, and elms, it was where all the neighborhood action took place: the football games, the safaris, the chase-and-fights. We built forts in the wild sumac and plum thickets and played among the ancient ruins: cairnlike street markers, a slouching gazebo, and the shallow, busted-up dish of a concrete fountain pool. I sometimes wonder if this is what initially attracted me to our current property in Council Bluffs, which is littered with crumbling retaining walls and stone steps and even the partially exposed ridge of an old concrete wading pool. I think I may have had a vision of our future children turning over those broken chunks to find, as I once had, hidden galaxies of creepy-crawly life.

The Kelley house seemed like a mansion to me: five bedrooms, a playroom over the garage, miles of crawl space, and a dumbwaiter. During that first tour, when we went upstairs to check out the bedrooms, I immediately called the one with the two huge closets and private bathroom. Mom explained that the bedrooms had already been assigned, and mine was down the hall. When I first saw it, my heart sank—it was small and dim and smelled like the old hat boxes in my great-aunt Esther's attic. And there was no private bathroom. Then I noticed the mysterious door, under which leaked what looked suspiciously like sunlight. Mrs. Kelley yanked it open, and it was as if I'd stepped into a dream: a sleeping porch! The wall-to-wall windows were cranked wide to let in the spring breeze and the sharp-edged scent of a blue spruce towering outside, its branches scraping against the screens. It felt like a tree house.

As a bonus, the porch was crammed full with stuff some adult must have thought useless junk but which I considered treasure: a crumpled poster of a toreador fighting a bull, a disassembled BB gun, a unicycle, a metal bunk-bed frame, and several half-crushed model airplanes whose condition appeared salvageable. But what really caught my eye was the dead fox resting on the tattered velvet of an old sofa. The fox was dusty and missing a leg—it had been mounted with wire, some of which was exposed—yet the way its black lips peeled back over its yellow fangs suggested a still smoldering, rabid fierceness.

I picked it up, set it on the bedroom floor, and asked if I could keep it.

"Well," Mrs. Kelley replied, "you'll have to talk to Pat and Pete. They killed the awful thing."

She might as well have told me to climb Mount Olympus. Pat and Pete were her twin sons, tall and slender, with fine blond hair hanging over their ears. Teenagers, they never played with any of us younger boys. Never talked to us. I admired and feared them for that, as I did most of the older boys in the neighborhood, boys who'd become one in my mind with the sounds of slamming car doors and revving engines and the loud, knowing laughter that seemed to carry them and their girlfriends down my street at night.

But with the Kelley twins there'd been something more, something about their solidarity as brothers that held me in awe. One afternoon, between that first tour of the house and when we actually moved there, I stood on the fence separating our yards and watched them play basketball in the driveway. They were shirtless, even in March, shuffling and slapping at each other's pale arms. At one point they stopped playing and sat down together on the front steps of my soon-to-be home. They stayed there, panting, until one of them got up, went inside, and returned with two bottles of pop. They took a few swigs and leaned back into the sun. Then they were at it again, their thin bodies slicing into each other, blond hair dancing, their huffy curses floating over to me like news from a distant radio.

That's how I always imagined it would be with a brother. Standing together, towering above the lone boys like me, never needing more than each other.

I stepped down from the fence—there was no room for anyone else in that story. It had been ridiculous for Mrs. Kelley to think I could just trot up and ask them for their fox, their trophy, interrupting the powerful force that was now and always passing between them. Yet I held tight to the larger dream. From the very beginning, Mom's pregnancy and the promise of a new house had meant, to me, the promise of a new brother. Watching the Kelley twins, week after week, there seemed no other way to live there but with another boy.

After hauling the final, supersized suitcase up to my old bedroom, I limped downstairs and asked when Grandma K was going to arrive. Mom said she'd just called to say she was too tired, but would be joining us the next day for church and Easter dinner. I was both relieved and disappointed. I wasn't sure I was quite ready to face my grandmother under these newly terminal conditions. On the other hand, I was desperate to see her that weekend and for Ben and Spencer to see her. It might be our last holiday together.

Thinking about that impending loss had inspired me, before leaving Council Bluffs, to drag out a weathered photo album of our first year in the Kelley house. The pictures of Christmas Day 1974 were filled with relatives, now gone or about to be gone. Grandma K and Grandpa Andy. Aunt Esther (Andy's older sister) and her husband, Leonard. Grandma Mildred and Grandpa Roy. Only two of them remained: Grandma K and Aunt Esther, who resided in a nearby nursing home and had trouble remembering who she was. The men were the first to go, with Grandpa Roy and Uncle Leonard both dying of heart attacks. A couple of years after that Christmas gathering, Grandpa Andy would suffer his stroke in Arizona. He died in 1998.

In the holiday photos, these men were still larger than life: big-boned, with towering, angular frames that carried serious weight, both literal and symbolic. In one snapshot, colossal Uncle Leonard, with his bristling white flat-top, is bent over a card table, intent on defeating me at our new air hockey game, which I'm sure he did—no freebies from those guys.

"It's the way of the world," they'd told me more than once after winning away all my pennies during card games.

But the presence of these men and women had ultimately served not as an introduction to the real world but as protection from it. Beneath that rooftop of giants, childhood imagination and dream had safely flourished, free of worldly concerns. Even today, when I feel overwhelmed by grown-up responsibilities, I sometimes find myself returning to those days with them, and can almost feel their arms lifting me beyond worry. It seems to me now an antiquated extravagance, to be enfolded during childhood by such a large and intimate number of ancestors. An extravagance I wanted my own children to enjoy, if only for a brief time, as insurance against the future.

After dinner, Ben and Spencer got busy dying eggs. They plopped the colored tablets into coffee mugs filled with vinegar and water, where they sizzled and dissolved like some ancient alchemy, which it sort of was. That bubbly, smelly concoction would ultimately transform something that came out of a chicken's filthy cloaca into something beautiful, something worth seeking and finding and hoarding. But *never* eating—my mother was positively paranoid about Easter eggs, never allowing anyone to consume them for fear of salmonella. Consequently, my sisters and I had ended up keeping the decorated eggs in our bedrooms until they got salmonella proper.

No one ever had to worry about starving at my mother's house, however. Before Ben and Spencer headed up to bed, she gave them each their usual "snack pack" of M&M's, Cap'n Crunch's Peanut

Butter Crunch cereal, popcorn, and blueberry mini-muffins—one of the many ritual indulgences never occurring in their own home. There would've been a movie or two or three popped into their bedside VCR, except that, as my mother emphasized, the Easter Bunny was on his way.

That night, while almost everyone else was asleep, I got to work. I'd encouraged Steph to get some rest, since the boys would likely be up at dawn to hunt eggs—she enjoyed being the one to hide them in the yard. I'd always enjoyed staying up late to distribute the goodies, though Easter wasn't exactly my favorite holiday. That evening, there was some pleasure in knowing the holiday magic would be occurring for my children in the very place I'd experienced it as a child. At the same time, it was impossible to escape memories of the Easter night when that magic officially ended for me.

My brother, James, was stillborn the night of Good Friday, 1974. In the morning, our father gathered my sisters and me on their bed to tell us the sad news. I don't remember much of what he said, only that an hour or so later I was leaning over the back of our couch, looking out the window at the rain. Later that evening, Mrs. Freeburg, our babysitter and one of Grandma K's best friends, attempted to scratch together the holiday for my sisters and me. We dyed eggs for the Easter Bunny to hide and fought as usual over the colors and stickers and wire egg dippers. When that was finished, Mrs. Freeburg herded us quickly from table to TV, and put a bowl of popcorn in each of our laps, as if to anchor our bodies, as well as our spirits, in place. On the screen rolled the second half of *The Ten Commandments,* as it had almost every Easter weekend. The message was clear: Nothing had changed. Except she'd forgotten things, like how much death there is in that movie. Together we watched God bring down one plague after another on the Egyptians, culminating in the deaths of their firstborn sons, including Pharaoh's son.

So many children dying.

Even so, I felt comforted by the story. We're not as bad as

Pharaoh, I thought, so our punishment couldn't possibly be the same. To lose a child, a boy, as he had.

A few hours later I lay in my top bunk and prayed, something along the lines of: *Didn't you part the sea for Moses? Didn't you make your son Jesus rise up from the dead?* Assurances seemed to leak through the cracked window—the smell of wet earth and grass and, after a winter locked indoors, the sounds of the neighborhood at night: the buzz of a streetlamp, the pulsing hiss of traffic, the yowl of a tomcat. In that season, as in all the sudden seasons of Iowa, I might wake to find the world dressed in something completely new. Snow or frost or flowers. Why not my own life?

Eventually I heard car wheels splash through a puddle, the crunch of wet gravel, and the familiar growl of our Buick. Dad was home from the hospital. I heard the front door jimmy open, some mumbling with Mrs. Freeburg, then the tinkle of plates and silverware, the smell of food—a late supper. I could almost see him, his forearms resting on the table, using his wrists to lift the food to his lowered head. "That's the Price way," Grandma K would've scolded, "dropping your head like a dog to the bowl. The civilized way is to lift the fork all the way to your mouth." But Grandma wasn't there, nor had she or any of my grandparents visited us during the day. No one had. It was a holiday empty of these grown-up relatives—a foreshadowing of my future.

When Dad finished his meal, I heard him push his chair back from the table and walk to the bottom of the stairs. There was the rustle of something plastic, the groan of a stair step, and then the sound of things dropping on the carpet: *pat, pat, pat.* He climbed another few steps and stopped: *pat, pat, pat.* At the top of the stairs, he turned and walked toward my sisters' bedroom. *Pat, pat, pat. Pat, pat, pat.* A few seconds later, he appeared in my doorway. The hallway light was on, and I could see a bit of messed-up hair on the side of his head and the wrinkled edge of his dress shirt. I was staring right at him, but he didn't see me. Which was good because he'd become a stranger. Something about the way he stood there, looking at the floor, shoulders slouched, hands fumbling with a plastic bag like he was just another clumsy, exhausted child. Not a grown man. Not my father.

He removed his fist from the bag and I saw that it was full of little candy bars, which he let drop, one by one by one—*pat, pat, pat*—onto the floor, hitting the lip of the slippers I'd left outside my door for the Easter Bunny.

And then I knew.

Thirty-two years later, in my parents' living room, I put the finishing touches on a small Easter display for my own children. Two chocolate bunnies, a couple of toys, a bug identification book, and a rake. The windows were open just a crack, letting in the same smell of wet earth and grass. My father, who had been dozing in the family room, came up and put his arm around my shoulder.

"How wonderful," he said.

The next morning, the boys rushed downstairs, stuffing tiny candy bars and jellybeans into their mouths along the way. After admiring the Easter Bunny's brilliant arrangement of candy and gifts, they grabbed their wicker baskets—the same ones my sisters and I had used—and headed outdoors. Stephanie was notorious for hiding eggs in the most difficult places. This time, the boys were forced to retrieve them from inside a remnant raspberry bramble, a dank gutter-spout, the charred interior of the cast-iron grill, and the spiky branches of the hawthorn tree. This resulted in some minor injuries, some bleeding, but nothing dampened their enthusiasm for finding every single egg.

Later that morning, Ben and Spencer didn't demonstrate nearly as much enthusiasm for sitting still in church. Despite Grandma K's stern looks, they squirmed and sighed and accidentally kicked the pew in front of them with the cowboy boots their Grandpa Tom had given them. This prompted the occupants to turn around and flash false smiles, but Steph had prepared for this inevitability and quickly disseminated the crayons and coloring books. Grandma was not amused.

"Time was when children paid attention in church."

Yes, I wanted to reply, *and time was when children mined coal and scrubbed the insides of industrial chimneys.* I flashed my own false smile instead and reached for her hand. She returned her attention to the minister's sermon on Christ's resurrection. Her face offered few clues as to what she was thinking in that moment, how she might be responding to the theology laid out before her, the mystery she might soon be confronting firsthand. She sat straight-backed and dignified in the pew. Although a little gaunt, her face was, as always, tastefully made up, a touch of rose on her lips and on her high, striking cheekbones. She'd been a beauty once, an occasional model, and still took care with her appearance.

Watching her, I assumed my grandmother's thoughts were probably focused on something sad, some lost loved one or disappointed desire or ongoing grudge—perhaps the fact that I didn't visit her enough. Did she feel unwanted? Is that why she was checking out? Now I recognize the arrogance in these thoughts, the assumption that my grandmother found meaning and happiness only inside our attention. She was ninety-two, and so much of her life had been spent beyond us, before us. Who knew which life was at the front of her mind in those moments during Easter service, which thoughts and feelings? Which reasons?

Back at the house, there was no opportunity to talk with Grandma or anyone else about her decision. As my mother busily prepared dinner, Grandma took her usual spot on the couch by the fireplace. She was quickly joined by the boys showing off their individual eggs, as well as each toy, book, and piece of candy: "Here's a peanut butter egg, Gramma K, and here's another peanut butter egg, and here's a rake and here's . . ."

"Gee whiz," she commented. "Kids sure get a lot of gifts for Easter these days. If I'd known that, I'd have gotten you something too, but I'm not sure your Grandma Sondra could have found the time to drive me to the store. Ever since I was forced to give up my driver's license, I don't get out much."

This went over the heads of Ben and Spencer, but I saw the

pained look on my mother's face as she set a casserole on the table. Despite all the talk about my mother being a saint, Grandma didn't hesitate to send the occasional verbal arrow into her rib cage. Or anyone else's. Like another saint we knew, Grandma had long been adept at keeping a list of other people's failings, often reciting from it during casual conversations and family gatherings. It would usually begin with a straightforward statement like "You know I worship your mother"—then quickly veer south—"but I'd be lying if I said I wasn't hurt when she sold my mother's oak table at that garage sale." That garage sale was in 1975. We all had our own naughty list, ready for her to pull out at a moment's notice. Our transgressions seemed only to be growing, like the years.

In a way, it was comforting to know the possibility of sudden death had not changed her in this regard. I was still relieved when Ben and Spencer returned her attention to the candy and gifts. The last item they showed her was the plastic carton of "Resurrection Eggs" my mother had secretly slipped into their Easter Bunny pile that morning. Of all the bizarre combinations of Christian and pagan ritual to be observed on that holiday, this took top prize. Inside the carton were twelve brightly colored plastic eggs, each containing a small artifact from the biblical crucifixion narrative: a goblet for the last supper, a crown of thorns, a nail, dice, a spear, and so on.

I guess one had to admire the attempt to insert a bit of fun into the story of Christ's despair, torture, and execution.

Spencer cracked open the first egg and handed Grandma K a little plastic donkey. As she read to them from the accompanying booklet about Jesus' entrance into Jerusalem—"'Isn't it exciting that the donkey's owner freely gave the donkey when he found out it was for Jesus?'"—I tried to put cynicism aside and appreciate the scene before me. How many times had Grandma read to me as a child? Countless. She did so now with her usual enthusiasm and precise enunciation, earning their full attention. Earlier I'd hoped for the distraction of their young cousins, but then this moment might never have happened. Ben was especially enjoying it. He handed her the crown of thorns, impatient to get to the most exciting part of the Easter story, the bloody part. She read the corresponding text: "'They decided that if Jesus was really God, He would save himself from having to die. But Jesus had made it clear to the people that the Father's plan was not what they expected or wanted.'"

How would I tell them? I asked myself, once again. Then it occurred to me that maybe it wasn't my question to answer. In all the avoidance and worry over how to explain Grandma K's decision to our children, I hadn't considered the possibility that she might have something to say to them about it. And that it might be her right to say it first.

An hour or so later, my mother pulled me aside and asked if I'd mind taking Grandma home. I helped her with her coat and everyone came over to give her a hug. After assisting her down the front steps, she waited patiently outside our car while I cleared the mess of toys and children's CDs off of the dashboard, brushed the fishy crackers and Teddy Grahams off the seat, and removed the juice boxes from the floor. Finally, there was enough room for her in the passenger seat. When she sat down, there was a crunch.

"I won't even ask what that was," she said.

As I escorted her inside the front doors of Friendship Haven, I noticed many of the residents' windows were decorated with cutout eggs and bunnies—apparently, children weren't the only ones attracted to the festive, pagan sheen of the holiday. Grandma's door was decorated with a wreath of faux lilies, but near the threshold, on the floor, were a couple of toy Chihuahuas. One of them sported a Santa hat and sang "Feliz Navidad" when you squeezed its ear. Ben and Spencer had saved it from one of their kid's meals and given it to her for Christmas. It had been guarding her apartment ever since.

Grandma's real Chihuahua, Niña, began barking as soon as she put the key in the door, darting out to circle between her legs, and furiously wagging her tiny fan tail.

"See how she misses me?" Grandma said, picking her up. "Thanks for the ride, sweetie."

When she embraced me with her free arm, Niña growled a little. I ignored the threat and looked over Grandma's shoulder into the apartment. It was bright and spacious and immaculate, with a plush floral couch and matching armchairs. A lighted china cabinet stood in the corner, displaying her collection of Lalique crystal songbirds and decorative plates and Lladró figurines and two blue-green glass ducks I'd always admired as a child. Next to the cabinet stood her artificial ficus tree, its leaves and branches sparkling with tiny white lights. Through her picture window I could see the blossoming crab-apple saplings, their trunks still wrapped in protective orange plastic. The paper hearts Ben and Spencer had sent her for Valentine's Day remained taped to the window, as promised.

"I'd invite you to come in for a while, but you need to get home to your family," Grandma said. She pulled back a little and looked up at me. "Easter is hard for you, isn't it?"

The question caught me off guard.

"I think of him too this time of year," she continued. "I need to tell you something about that, but not right now."

Before I had time to ask what she meant, she pulled me into her arms again. I was relieved, to tell the truth; I wanted to get on the road well before dusk, when the deer came out. Now I wish I'd spent more of the afternoon with her, as I wish I'd spent more time with her in general. It was a gift I hardly recognized, even then, inside her embrace. To be almost forty and have my grandmother with me on Easter.

To still be someone's grandchild.

During the car trip back to Council Bluffs, while I puzzled over the weekend, Ben and Spencer were in the backseat decorating their empty Easter egg cartons. They once again planned to use them for their "Bug Collections." During the previous year, all sorts of things had ended up in those cartons: dried cicada nymphs and stray butterfly wings and spider egg sacs and still-active wasp nests, as well as noninsect items, such as buckeyes and bone bits and chocolaty, marblelike deer turds.

Many of the items the boys had collected were not traditionally considered "nature," unless one made no distinction (as they didn't) between the body and its natural environment. Especially fascinating were the aging bodies of their parents and grandparents and great-grandparent. For a while, our stray toenail clippings had been all the rage, then stubble out of my electric razor, then Steph's plucked eyebrow hairs. Spencer had once asked Grandma K if he could use scissors to cut off one of her wrinkles, and when a suspicious mole had been removed from my back for some testing, Ben was disappointed I hadn't saved it for his egg carton. Even the neighbor kids had gotten involved in building the collections, donating specimens of various worth and decay. One of them brought over a fifty-dollar bill and an unopened can of beer, which, he stressed, his dad considered very valuable items.

"Do you remember the Question Mark?" Ben asked Spencer in the backseat.

"Oh, yeah!"

The previous April, Ben had found a small chrysalis beneath the mulberry tree in the backyard. It was brown and dry, seemingly beyond hope. Ben insisted we give it a chance, so Steph glued it to the lid of a peanut butter jar and set it aside in the kitchen. A week or so later, a large butterfly emerged with irregularly edged, brown-and-bronze wings. It looked like a living leaf. We used our guide to identify it as an anglewing commonly called Question Mark for the silvery punctuation on the underside of its wing. It is one of the few resident butterflies to overwinter in our harsh climate, though how they pull that off is still a mystery.

"Question Marks have wings and can fly to the sun when it snows," Ben had hypothesized.

After that butterfly's seemingly miraculous resurrection, Steph and I endured several weeks of "I told you so!" Ben reminded us of it again in the car:

"Remember when you thought the Question Mark was dead, and it wasn't?"

Spencer chimed in with his own recollections of creatures his parents had mistakenly assumed deceased: roly-polies, mice, crickets, and a nasty mud dauber wasp that suddenly woke up and stung me on the palm of the hand.

"I told you Muddy was alive," Spencer scolded me again from his thronelike car seat. "But you didn't listen. You need to listen better."

"That's probably true," I said. Steph smiled.

"It's kinda tricky, Dad," Ben added. "You find something for your Bug Collection and sometimes you think it's dead, but it isn't. That makes it kinda hard to choose what to keep and what to let go."

"Yeah," Spencer agreed. "That's the hardest part."

5

Night Comes for the
Brown Recluse

THE WEEK AFTER we returned home from Easter, I thought a little physical labor in the yard would take my mind off other stresses, but then I remembered it was our yard. For me, the experience of yard work is a little like the stages of grief. First, there is Denial (*This can't be happening to me—the grass couldn't have grown six inches in a week!*); then Anger (*Why can poison ivy only be destroyed by a precision nuclear missile strike?*); Bargaining (*I will live a life dedicated to God if my sons can be magically transformed into teenagers capable of pushing a lawn mower.*); Depression (*Why bother?*); and finally, Acceptance (*I can't fight it, so where's that beer the neighbor kid brought over?*).

I took a walk around the grounds, tallying up the score, and concluded I was hopelessly outmatched. And it was only April! I felt the opening shot of Anger, quickly ran through the other stages, but before landing helplessly on Acceptance, I noticed the golden glow along the far western border of the yard. Last fall, in a fit of botanical nostalgia, I'd planted around a dozen daffodils, their shoots having been one of the first signs of spring in my own childhood yard. I think planting this flower also had something to do with that scene in the movie *Doctor Zhivago* when the poet emerges from the brutal Russian winter into fields full of their yellow blossoms. I sometimes fancied myself a Zhivago, but without the girlfriend on the side and (hopefully) the paper-thin heart.

In any case, the glow drew me to the overgrown area along the old wood-board fence, its white paint weathered and cracked. It was probably fifty years old at least. The daffodils had been blooming there for a while, and I noticed their buttery edges were beginning to caramelize. It wouldn't be long before they vanished, and as if to emphasize the point, the black and indigo wings of a mourning cloak butterfly lighted on one of the blossoms.

But there were other plants to appreciate, ones not in the final throes of glory. Here and there, the Solomon's seals were uncurling themselves like lizard tongues and the broad, mushroomlike leaves of the bloodroot were poking through the wet layers of leaves. Bloodroot was another favorite plant from my childhood, and these had been transplanted from my mother's garden. Unlike the daffodil, bloodroot was a native woodland plant, and my buddies and I had often sought it out during hikes and campouts, breaking off the stems and using the reddish sap to draw battle wounds on our faces and arms. I had shown my boys and their friends how to do the same.

I decided that although I couldn't possibly tackle the entire yard that afternoon, I could at least clean up this sentimental spot. It wasn't much, but if I really was going to change my ways of looking at life, that effort would have to start here, at home. I'd long considered phrases like "living in the moment" and "appreciating the small things in life" to be frothy clichés. Standing in that quiet corner of the yard, however, they seemed to offer new possibilities, new *substance*.

I bent down, put my hand in the cold leaves, and felt the sun on my neck.

Like all yard work, no matter how modest, it turned out to be a bigger, dirtier job than expected. Still, I felt surprisingly satisfied when, hours later, I headed upstairs with aching legs—I think I'd forgotten I actually had muscles. A hot shower would feel wonderful. I pulled back the shower curtain and was getting ready to step into the tub, when I noticed a dark spot where I was about to put my foot. Closer inspection revealed it to be a large spider.

Finding large spiders in the bathtub was nothing unusual. We suspected they came out of the overflow drain and became trapped by the slippery porcelain walls. We suspected this because they'd sometimes crawled out of the drain when we were still in the tub. A couple of years ago, I was giving Spencer a bath when a huge wolf spider emerged from the overflow drain a few inches from his face. It was the size of a man's hand—at least that's how I remember it—and I instinctively jerked away. This spooked Spencer, who was one and a half at the time, and he started screaming and frantically trying to get out of the tub. While trying to prevent Spencer from hurting himself, we both fell onto the slippery floor, writhing as if in harmonious seizure.

Ben and Stephanie were quickly on the scene. Ben was thrilled when I pointed out the giant arachnid, and even Spencer, once he recovered himself, smiled at it from the safety of his mother's arms. We retrieved an empty peanut butter jar and, after a few deft maneuvers with a piece of paper, "Teddy" the wolf spider became the newest member of the family.

Like the mice, we eventually set Teddy free, but the experience made the boys lifelong fans of spiders. Especially Ben. During visits to the library, he would gather all the spider-related books he could carry, sit down at one of the children's tables, and peruse the pictures. His favorite was *The World of the Spider* by Adrienne Mason. This scrapbook of horrors included close-up photographs of mating nursery-web spiders, dozens of newly hatched spiderlings riding on their mother's hairy back, a pile of beetle heads scattered outside a wolf spider's den, an orb weaver snacking on a honey bee, a swarm of social spiders feasting on a moth, and a ghost-white wheel spider devouring a gecko. Out of fairness, I suppose, the author also included a photo of a pompilid wasp laying her eggs on a wheel spider's paralyzed body, where the offspring would eventually hatch and devour it alive.

At the library, as Ben exclaimed loudly over these morbid photos, we got more than one critical look from patrons whose children were trying to enjoy *The Poky Little Puppy* or *Hop on Pop*.

But Ben was right—the world of spiders is pretty amazing, full of beauty and diversity as well as danger and death. Thanks to that world, Ben began approaching our own with a new sense of wonder. The basement, for instance. Before Ben's interest in spiders, the basement of our old house had been the habitat of only nightmares, a place to be avoided at all costs. I couldn't have agreed more—it was dark, dank, and cluttered. If you died down there, you might not be discovered for days.

After watching me swat my way through a giant web at the top of the basement stairs, Ben changed his tune. Whenever I was forced to go down there, which thankfully was rare, Ben would insist on going with me, toting his Elmo flashlight and an antique magnifying glass I'd inherited from Uncle Leonard. In the basement, he located and studied, among other specimens, huge house spiders with bulbous abdomens and audaciously painted tattoos and wispy cellar spiders with delicate, nearly invisible legs. Egg sacs were of particular interest, especially in the middle of hatching when the tiny spiderlings, spreading out from the white core, resembled the cosmic birth of stars.

So when it came to this latest specimen in the bathtub, there was no question what Ben would want me to do. I thought about the writing I needed to get done and my aching muscles and the hassle of locating a container, and seriously considered the more expedient response: squashing it with a wad of tissue and flushing the evidence down the toilet. But then I imagined the excitement, the joy in Ben's face when his father showed him the magnificent spider he'd captured. I stepped downstairs and returned with an empty peanut butter jar and a piece of paper.

We had, by that time, perfected this particular technique of capture-and-release, one of the many here in the No-Kill Zone. As usual, I used my finger to try to scare the spider onto the paper, but he did not appear intimidated. Finally, I touched one of its long, jointed legs and it scurried into position. I carefully put the jar on top of it, then realized I'd neglected to bring a lid. No matter. I carefully slipped my hand beneath the paper, trying not to let the spider escape under the rim, which it almost did, and placed the jar on top of the stair banister. This was my first chance to really study the creature. I didn't recognize the species—it was silver-dollar-sized, with a small tannish body and unusually long legs. I thought it might be some version of a nursery web spider, a species we'd seen in the yard a couple of times. I left it there and took my shower.

Hours later, as I was getting into the car to go to the store, I remembered the spider.

"Hey, you guys!" I called to Ben and Spencer, who were playing nearby. "Come inside—I have a surprise for you."

Steph joined us and we all rushed upstairs to the peanut butter jar, still resting on the banister.

"Whoa! Thanks, Dad!" Ben exclaimed. "What kind of spider is *that*?"

The look on his face was everything I'd hoped for.

"I think it's a nursery web spider."

"Uh, John," Steph said. "That looks like it might be a brown recluse."

"No way," I said.

"*Way*. Look at the fiddle mark on its back."

Sure enough—*How could I have missed it?* Brown recluses are the most venomous spider in North America, but they're more common farther south. I'd never seen one, ever, which may explain why I'd scooted it around with my finger and then left it under a peanut butter jar perched precariously at the top of the stairs, where any one of us could have knocked it over.

My first thought was I should've killed it when I had the chance—*This is what I get for being an attentive father!* I casually tried to step away to find the cotton balls and alcohol.

"Where are you going?" Ben asked.

"Uh, just looking for a book."

"But there aren't any books in the medicine cabinet."

I broke down and told them the truth. "Don't kill Brownie!" Spencer yelled, tears welling.

"*Brownie?*" I responded. "This isn't *Brownie,* this is a deadly spider! It could kill you!"

"That's not Brownie's fault!" Ben joined in. "God made him that way!"

"Right, and God also made rabid bats and Gila monsters, but are we going to keep them as pets?" I looked at Steph, who is no fan of spiders, but she was clearly as enthralled by the recluse as they were.

"OK," I said, "but before you decide to invite this thing into our home, I want you to see something."

We marched downstairs to the computer, where I quickly downloaded dozens of photos of brown recluse bites, everything from the circular marking of an early wound to the gaping, bloody, tennis-ball-sized hole where the flesh had rotted away. One victim looked like half his face had melted off.

"Get a load of that, people," I said, convinced by the open-mouthed stares that I'd won the day.

"Cool!" Ben said. "Can I take these pictures to school to show my friends?"

It was over. Brownie was destined to become the latest arachnid to join the clan. We explained to the boys, however, that when it came to the recluse, there could never be any "born free" moment. He would live and die inside that peanut butter jar. I also hoped Brownie would remain our little family secret, but when you're harboring the most venomous spider in North America, word spreads quickly among neighborhood children. Kids we hadn't seen in months, or didn't recognize at all, showed up at our door to see the monster. Several curious parents showed up as well, interested, I'm sure, in seeing the kind of parents who would allow their children to keep such a thing on their kitchen counter. When Ben asked one of his friends to stay for a sleepover, we had to assure his nervous mother that the house wasn't infested with deadly arachnids. We'd actually checked out this possibility with a recluse expert at a university, who confirmed it was a brown recluse—a rare sighting in Iowa—and assured us it probably was just chased indoors by spring rains. They prefer the outdoors and will normally stay clear of people. If the house was infested, we would have seen more of them by now.

"Of course," he wrote in his e-mail, "there aren't any guarantees."

What could we do? Life and sleepovers had to go on.

Ben and his friends regularly brought Brownie live crickets and other small bugs, though none of them had the stomach to watch him actually kill and eat them—a good sign, I thought, that they wouldn't grow up to be serial killers. During the day, Brownie hid under a piece of bark we'd placed in his jar, but evidence that he was enjoying his nocturnal meals could be seen everywhere. To my surprise, no one expressed concern that sacrificing the crickets was a violation of the No-Kill Law. As Ben put it, Brownie would have been eating bugs in the yard anyway. Spencer didn't say anything either, though he refused to participate in the capture of crickets or watch as they were placed in the peanut butter jar or count the number of cricket legs piling up in the bottom, which Ben did on a regular basis. Spencer eventually stopped looking at the jar altogether, which we interpreted as indifference.

But Spencer was far from indifferent. Over the week or so we'd been housing and feeding Brownie, Spencer's sympathies apparently had been shifting. He would later confess that the spider had been increasingly "getting on my nerds." Although he didn't want

Brownie killed, he didn't like it that he was eating so many crickets. He wondered why Brownie didn't at least try a little of the grass and bark we put in there. He might even like them, he said, just like the guy with the green eggs and ham.

"And Brownie's a bully," Spencer added.

Ben had recently told him all about bullies, how they pick on kids littler than they are. From Spencer's point of view, Brownie fit the bill. Indeed, the crickets had all been undersized and hopelessly outmatched. It *was* unfair.

Then one evening, Spencer came in with his collecting jar and announced he had a "present" for Brownie. Inside the jar was the biggest cricket we'd ever seen—midnight black and covered with rhino armor, its thick legs impressively serrated. The Darth Vader of crickets. Spencer had already named him "Jiminy," which made his willingness to sacrifice him to the spider perplexing. Apparently, Spencer sensed something about the cricket we did not. Ben was more than willing to oblige. This was the equivalent of a twenty-five-pound Thanksgiving turkey, and Ben, being a big eater himself, figured Brownie would be more than grateful to receive it. So he carefully opened the lid and Spencer dropped Jiminy inside. Before we left, we thought we saw a long brown leg extend from beneath the bark.

The next morning, Steph and I were still in bed when we heard shouting. We both rushed downstairs and found Ben and Spencer in the kitchen. Ben was pointing at the peanut butter jar, tears streaming down his face.

"He killed him! He killed him!"

We looked inside, expecting to see the remains of Jiminy. Instead, the massive black cricket was perched on the broken remains of the most venomous spider in North America. I couldn't believe it, and I'm sure poor Brownie had also been surprised. I tried to imagine the stages of grief he must have experienced, beginning with the initial denial, something along the lines of "*Oh my God*, I can't believe I'm being killed by a freaking cricket!"

Ben was going through a few of those stages himself, but not

Spencer. He stood a little ways off with a small, almost indiscernible smile on his face. Balance had been restored to the universe, or at least to our kitchen. And something else as well: a new respect for the common cricket. Out of that respect, we decided to grant Jiminy his hard-earned freedom, but only after admiring him in the jar for a few days. At first, Ben couldn't feel anything but hatred for him, but soon he grudgingly gave in to awe. As did his friends, who after hearing the story came over to see Jiminy in numbers even greater than to see Brownie. This was not the Jiminy of their fathers' and grandfathers' generations, playing a fiddle and wishing on a star. This was a dark warrior beyond imagining who, for days afterward, posed triumphantly on the piece of bark that had once been the lair of his now-vanquished enemy.

In the evenings, after all the lights were turned out, his boastful chirping was loud enough to be heard in the upstairs bedrooms. For those who were unable to sleep, because of thoughts or worries or whatever, it was annoying at first. But then it became a kind of rare and comforting song. I listened for it every night, even after the so-called insect had returned to the wilds of our overgrown yard.

Do not be afraid, it seemed to say, *I am Jiminy, the slayer of fear, the conqueror of death. Hear me and rejoice!*

6

Trap-Door Spider Lair

I CLEARED THE RUBBLE off the couch and collapsed for what I hoped would be a quick nap. It was around noon, and I had been up most of the night working on the novel, but that was just a detail—since becoming parents, Steph and I seemed to be in a perpetual state of sleep deprivation. We weren't alone. A friend of mine, who was also a father, once said that parents hunt for naps like great white sharks hunt for seals—relentlessly, viciously. My seal was now in sight. The kids were outside and Steph was writing a paper for her distance learning class on the computer in the laundry nook. She'd asked if I wouldn't like to spend some time with the boys in the woods, but I wasn't about to waste this rare, quiet atmosphere on anything but REM. I pulled the sofa blanket over my head, shut my eyes, and drifted off.

The phone rang.

"It's Grandma K," Steph called from the kitchen.

I gave her an annoyed look as she handed me the phone. "Hello, Grandma."

"You could put a little more effort into that greeting," she replied. "Were you just lying down for a nap?"

"Uh, yes."

"I thought so. This is about the time your grandfather always took a nap on Saturdays. 'The lord's day,' he called it. Lord with a small 'l.'" She laughed while Niña barked in the background.

"I'm giving her her doggy treats—*yes I am, aren't I, you wittle cutie-patootie*. I just *wuv* this dog, John. Anyway, I won't bother you for long. Are the boys there? I've been thinking about them today."

"You're not bothering me . . ." I said, then felt the panic rise as I considered she might be planning to tell Ben and Spencer about her decision. Before I could worry much further, Ben ran in and reached for the phone, closely followed by Spencer. Steph apparently had told them who was on the line.

"Hi, Gramma K!" Ben said, and began narrating his day, of which I could only discern a string of conjunctions: ". . . and . . . and . . . and . . . and . . . and. . . ." Even if she wanted to talk about something serious, it was going to be hard to get a word in edgewise.

I relaxed a little and lay my head back on the pillow. I quickly snapped to when I heard Spencer telling his great-grandmother about the new book Mommy had gotten him, called *Body Baddies: All About the Mini-Monsters Living on You!*

"It has a picture of a tapeworm, and it lives inside your *stomach*. Did *you* ever have a tapeworm living inside *your* stomach, Gramma?"

I didn't hear her response, but it made Spencer giggle.

"Love you, too," he said, and handed me the phone. "Gramma K wants to tell you something."

I winced, expecting to be scolded for what we allowed our children to read. Plenty of others had expressed concern, directly or indirectly, about the books we had laying around the house, books about venomous spiders and mythological monsters and animal skeletons and sword-making, to name just a few. Steph had ordered this latest masterpiece from a preschool book catalog because it seemed to cover a couple of Spencer's interests. Bugs, of course, but also human anatomy, which he'd seen illustrated in a children's science book his brother had checked out from the library. I think Spencer was fascinated by the idea that the body, like the dirt beneath a rock, contained a hidden universe.

But *Body Baddies* took that interest to a new level. A lower level. It included chapter titles such as "What Lives on Your Face?" and "What's Burrowing through Your Flesh?" and included close-up photographs of such lovelies as the botfly maggot ("nicely fat after chewing on human flesh"), the dust mite ("with some of its skin flake breakfast"), and a guinea worm being pulled from its "lair" inside someone's foot. When I'd questioned Steph's wisdom in ordering this book, she'd replied that she knew her boy. Indeed, Spencer had hardly put it down, begging us daily to read it to him. He'd also enthusiastically taken up the cause of educating others about the body as ecosystem, sometimes during dinner.

"Don't worry," Grandma K said to me, "I'm getting off the phone so you can get back to dreamland—that's your full-time job anyway, isn't it? I just wanted to say how adorable your boys are; they're so creative. *Tapeworms*, honestly. You should feel very proud of the family you and Stephanie are raising. And lucky—not everyone has a family like yours. I didn't."

"You're a big part of our family, Grandma."

"Well, you know I worship you," she said, and I braced for the turn south, but there wasn't one.

"Just do me a favor and be a good father to those boys, OK? Not like my father."

"OK," I replied. She was opening a door to a room she rarely visited, and I should have encouraged her to share more, but I was tired.

"Well, have a good nap," she said. "I love you."

"Love you, too." I hung up the phone, fell back onto the couch, and entered a fitful, unsatisfying sleep.

Not like my father. So who was her father, anyway? Grandma rarely mentioned him. From what I could gather, he was just a shadow figure during most of her childhood, animated only by the anger of her mother and grandmother, and later by the questions that seemed to haunt her life story: "Why?" and "What if . . . ?" Her father's irresponsible behavior seemed to have set in motion a series of disappointments that had perpetually stranded her just shy of contentment—the lonely childhood on her grandparents' farm, the stepfathers who had never done right by her, the inability to fully trust the love of others, especially men.

"She's never satisfied," my grandfather had once told me in frustration.

My family suspected much of it could be traced back to her father, to his choice to abandon her when she was just old enough to know it.

So who was Clifford Hobson? Grandma had offered some sketchy details: raised in Clifton, Illinois; college educated; star baseball player whose dreams of a pro career ended with an injury; employed as a mechanic in Lehigh (where he also played farm ball and met his wife, Nina Porter) and then by the Ford company in Chicago. Their first child, my grandmother, was born in the Hobson home in Clifton in 1914, and her sister, Virginia, was born a couple years later in Chicago. They lived in the Windy City for a few more years as a family until, at some point, Clifford purchased train tickets for Nina and their young daughters to visit her parents in Lehigh. He never sent money for their return.

Game over.

Grandma K couldn't remember what he looked like, only the sound of his voice through the heating vent at her grandparents' farmhouse. He apparently had come back to Lehigh and asked to see his daughters, but her Grandma Josephine demanded he buy them some new shoes first. He mumbled something, and she told him to get out. Afterward, she overheard her grandmother declare that if that man ever returned, she'd dump boiling water on him. He didn't. Since then, Clifford had become a faceless abstraction to his descendants. We'd seen no photos of him—Nina and/or Josephine had cut all of them out of Kathryn's childhood albums. He was just so much negative space, his sins not worth mentioning, because he wasn't worth mentioning.

Then, unexpectedly, he returned to us. To me.

When we moved Grandma from her apartment to Friendship Haven in 2002, we went through a box of moldy photos and papers in her basement. I discovered a negative of what looked to be a young couple sitting on the porch steps of a large house. Out of curiosity, I had it developed and saw my own face staring back at me. For a long time, I didn't think I really resembled anyone in our immediate family; I had been small and freckled with reddish-brown hair that curled when it grew out too long in the summers. This had been a source of some good-natured speculation among my sisters: Did Mom have an affair with the redheaded mailman? With Howdy Doody? With Ralph Malph from *Happy Days*?

As it turned out, I looked a lot like Grandma K's father, the long-lost Clifford C. "Red" Hobson. In the photo, he was dressed in a smart suit and was leaning casually against the stone balustrade of the porch steps, while a girlish Nina (I recognized her from other photos) leaned into him affectionately. On his face, my face, was the confident, almost smug grin of self-satisfied youth. He probably was in his mid-twenties when the picture was taken—how long had they been married? Were they married? Had my grandmother been born yet? Where was the picture taken?

Those were just a few of my questions. When I showed the photo to Grandma, her reaction was cool. She didn't know when it was taken or where, only that it wasn't any house she could remember from Lehigh. Perhaps it was her grandmother Hobson's place in Clifton, Illinois, where she'd been born.

I wanted to question her further, but something told me to lay off. It was frustrating. For years I hadn't cared enough to ask about

Clifford, but now that I saw his face, saw my own face in his, I felt the need to know more. It might help me better understand my grandmother's life, and also the mystery of my relationship with her. Maybe somewhere in her unconscious mind, her father's face and my face had become one. Is this why she'd always craved my attention? Why she'd so often treated me with blatant favoritism around the rest of the family? Why she'd expressed such unrealistically high expectations for my personal and professional success? She was heartbroken, for instance, when I told her during a visit to Arizona that I was abandoning my undergraduate studies in pre-medicine for a career in teaching literature and writing. Soon after, she took me on a tour of some of the wealthiest neighborhoods in Tucson.

"Do you like that house?" she asked, as I gawked at yet another huge adobe mansion. "Well, you'll never own it as a writer."

"You'd make such a *wonderful* doctor, John," she continued, almost pleading. "You'll heal so many people, truly help them, and make a lot more money besides. Wouldn't you and your future family enjoy a beautiful house like that one over there? You need to think of them, too. You could still do a little writing on the side. Everyone needs a hobby."

Even after completing my doctorate and landing the job in Omaha, she occasionally reminded me that it wasn't too late to apply to medical school and buy my deserving wife and kids the house of their dreams. I'd laughed off most of this nonsense, but it seemed that, against my will, I'd also internalized a lot of it. When I found that photo of my great-grandfather, I was still a couple years away from the heart-attack scare, but already well inside the unhealthy thoughts and behaviors. I could never do enough. I was never satisfied.

This might have been another, unconscious reason I had wanted to know more about Clifford. I perhaps worried, even then, that behind our similar faces there might lurk other similarities. Could shared physical characteristics, passed down from one generation to the next, also signify shared characteristics of mind? By knowing Clifford's life story, including his brief life as a father, might I also better understand my own?

These were questions I didn't think I'd have the chance to answer. Then, in the spring of 2004, I was invited to give a book reading at DePaul University in Chicago. We decided to bring the kids along for a mini-vacation, and then swing through Clifton on the way home to see what we could discover. The night after the reading, Steph and I went out to dinner with my college friend Michele, who is a professor at DePaul, and her partner, Kevin. While we all waited for the babysitter to arrive at the hotel, three-year-old Ben entertained Michele and Kevin with a dramatic rendition of the hunting techniques of the trap-door spider. By far his favorite photograph in *The World of the Spider* was the close-up of the trap-door spider, its two hairy legs extending from beneath the silky lid of its lair. The accompanying text, which he always begged us to read out loud, described the "ambush style" of these "sit-and-wait predators," how they "set up booby traps by creating silken trip wires" and spring with "lightning speed" onto their hapless prey. The leftover body parts of beetles, ants, and other unfortunates are kept in a webby bag outside the lair, which can be pulled over the entrance whenever the spider feels threatened.

We thought Ben's obsession with this creature was a private affair, until his preschool teachers nervously informed us that he'd invented a classroom game called "Trap-Door Spider Attack!" During free time one morning, Ben stacked a few play tires on top of one another, creating a "lair" where he could hide. Whenever a classmate wandered by, he would spring out at them, hissing. After the initial fright or two, all the kids lined up to take turns playing the spider and the prey—both roles having their appeal, apparently. Now, at the hotel, Ben used a pile of couch cushions and a pillow lid to demonstrate this game for Michele and Kevin, who, to their credit, found it far more amusing than the preschool teachers.

The morning of our departure, we got up early and headed to Clifton, just an hour and a half south of the city. When we reached the borders of the small farming community, it hit me that it was Sunday and there would be little chance of doing any family history research. We pulled up to the library, but it was closed. With nothing else to do, we drove around the town, past houses and churches, wondering if they had any family significance. We eventually turned onto a gravel road heading north of town. It was mostly fields, and we were about to turn back when we spotted an elderly woman riding a lawnmower in front of a large farmhouse. On a whim, I pulled over and waved. She turned off the mower and eyed me suspiciously. When I explained I was a descendant of the Hobsons and was looking for information about the family, her face brightened.

"I was wondering when one of you was going to show up. Come inside."

Her name was Norma, and she invited us to sit down at her kitchen table, where she served us lemonade and cookies. She said she was sort of the unofficial historian of Clifton, and that the Hobsons had once been a prominent family there.

"Now which Hobson are you related to?"

When I told her I was the great-grandson of Clifford, she raised her eyebrows.

"The baseball star? I didn't know he had any descendants, besides the daughter."

After I told her what I knew about the situation, she paused and asked Steph and the boys if they'd like some more lemonade. She refilled their glasses, but not mine.

"You come with me," she said.

Norma led me to a dark study where papers and boxes were piled on a large desk, spilling onto the floor. She cleared some manila envelopes off a chair and invited me to sit down. From one of the tall file cabinets, she retrieved an overstuffed accordion folder.

"I've been gathering this material on the Hobson family for years. Take a look."

Inside were hundreds of items: newspaper clippings of death announcements, anniversary and retirement celebrations, farm auctions, copies of marriage certificates, an old portrait painting of a mustached man, and near the bottom, a copy of Grandma Kathryn's birth certificate. It noted that she was "legitimate," that her parents were Clifford Carlton Hobson (age 24) and Nina Viola Porter (age 18), and was signed by Dora Hobson, witness and grandmother.

Norma returned to her computer and printed off several pages. It was the Hobson genealogical chart, and she walked me through the generations, from William Hobson, born in England in 1786, to Frank F. Hobson, the man in the painting, who was born in 1856. Frank was a successful local farmer who married Isadora "Dora" McCarl, daughter of another local farmer, and raised five children, including a son named Clifford. She pointed to his entry in the chart, which mentioned only that he was born in 1890, married Nina, had one child, Kathryn, and died in 1942.

"You can see I didn't have much information about him. Of course, I knew of him growing up, most people did around here, but his life has always been a bit of a mystery to me."

"You aren't the only one," I said. "I only recently discovered a photo of him. I don't even know where it was taken." I pulled it out of my book bag to show her.

"Why, that's the old Hobson home, just down the road from here. A nice young family lives there now, and I'm sure they wouldn't mind you visiting."

I then provided her with family names and information, which she typed into the chart, including what I knew about Grandma's sister Virginia's family in Canada. Clifford now had two daughters, two granddaughters, six great-grandchildren, and (at the time) ten great-great grandchildren. Norma made copies of all the relevant materials in the folder, but before she returned it to the cabinet, she took out the painting of Frank Hobson and handed it to me.

"Your family should have this. They should have something."

Outside, as we strapped the boys into their car seats, Norma repeated the directions to the Hobson home and to the cemetery, where she claimed we'd have no trouble finding the family plot. I thanked her profusely.

"I've got nothing to do with it. You were sent here by your ancestors, to claim them. The dead guide the living. I've experienced this kind of thing too many times not to know it."

It's a strange feeling arriving for the first time at a source of your existence. When I saw the large Victorian farmhouse come into view over the fields, I wondered if it really was the home where my great-grandfather had been raised, where he had brought his teenage bride, and where she had given birth to their daughter, my grandmother.

The question was answered the moment I saw the large wrap-around porch with the distinctive stone balustrades. The same as in the photo. We pulled into the drive, admiring the big yard full of towering maples and blooming redbuds and crab apples. The house was well maintained, painted bright salmon with white gingerbread trim. When I knocked on the front door, I could hear the familiar noise of young children playing inside. A man about my age answered, and after I told him my story, he and his wife brought out a framed photo of the house taken around the turn of the century. It looked the same, except the trees were barely more than saplings and the sky was more prominent. Someone had written "F. F. Hobson Residence" along the bottom edge. On the front porch steps, two young boys sat and gazed at the fields. One of them looked more than a little familiar.

I tried to imagine Clifford's boyhood spent in that beautiful house and yard, before the mess of later years—the evenings on the front porch with his family, the outdoor adventures with friends and siblings, and all the carefree, accidental fun I witnessed in my own boys' daily lives. What had happened to him?

A year or so later, I would have a better sense of the young man who became the father that abandoned my grandmother. When digging through yet another moldy box from Grandma's basement, I discovered a letter from Clifford's mother, Dora Mc-Carl Hobson. It was dated "May 12, 1942, Clifton, Ill" and had been sent to Kathryn on the occasion of her father's death, at age fifty-two, from throat cancer. Dora began by acknowledging she "always felt in a peculiar situation writing to you . . . I have always felt that you did not care to have Cliff mentioned." But now that "Cliff is gone I feel before I too am called away, I want to say, no matter who adopts or raises a child, blood will tell and you girls and your children after you, have no need to ever feel ashamed of your ancestors." She claimed the Hobsons were among "the highest and best families in their community," even though members of that family hadn't always done the right thing.

"Everyone makes mistakes," she added.

She went on to describe Clifford's funeral, how "such a gloom" settled over the community, how he had many friends and "was known far and wide from his ball playing days." Since he'd returned to Clifton five years prior, he'd umpired for high school games, organized an Old Time Ball Players reunion, and lived in the family home where "so many have said they thought so much of him for the way he has taken care of me." When it came to the obituary, however, she "felt you girls would not want to be mentioned so did not in any information I gave."

Dora described how much her son had suffered in the end from the cancer, but that he'd died peacefully. She concluded:

How I miss him no one can know. He would not go away [to the hospital] at first . . . I told him not to think about me, to think about himself. Finally he had to go. He took such pride in those two little baby pictures, he so rarely said any thing about his life, but he showed those pictures to friends and told them they were his grandchildren, and the pictures of you and Virginia.

Well Kathryn maybe I have done wrong to write this way to you, but most children do like to know something about their real blood parents. Cliff had too much freedom when he went away to school, he did not take responsibility. I often wish we had kept him home on the farm—he had a good intellect, read a good deal and was always well informed on most subjects. He could make a good appearance in the best of crowds. I just wanted to say this to pass down to the children in case they ever wanted to know what kind of families their ancestors were. I hope every one of you are well. . . . Give my love to every one and kiss the babies for me.

Lovingly
Grandmother Hobson

When I showed this letter to Grandma K, she vaguely remembered receiving it, but thought she had thrown it away. Perhaps Grandpa Andy had saved it. Rereading it did little to change her opinion of her father. She zeroed in on the part about how neither she nor Virginia had been mentioned in his obituary, and found little solace in the fact that he'd showed off pictures of his daughters and granddaughters.

"He never earned that right," she said, and handed the letter back to me.

My feelings about the letter were conflicted as well, but as I said to my mother and sisters, it offered a revealing context: Clifford's youthful irresponsibility, his local fame, his inability to adjust to life away from his rural home. Here, as well, was a family that had thought very highly of itself, that believed it held a prominent place in the community. What pressure had Clifford felt to live up to that reputation? In what ways, if any, had it moved him toward recklessness and rebellion—especially after the injury that ended his professional baseball dreams? At some point after leaving Nina and his daughters, he'd traveled to Lehigh to see them, but had been met at the door by another protective mother who sent him away. He eventually returned to his original family, his native community, and became part of them again. He took care of his widowed mother, even to the detriment of his own well-being—something his daughter Kathryn would do for many in her own family, including her mother.

Ultimately, I felt this final chapter in his life offered the possibility of partial redemption for Clifford by introducing a side of him none of us had known: his capacity to earn and give committed love.

But perhaps that was just wishful thinking.

Before leaving the Hobson home, the current owner took a picture of Steph and me and the boys sitting in the same spot where Clifford and Nina had once posed as a young couple. Even if Grandma didn't appreciate it, their love for one another, however brief, had continued to reverberate in the world, our world. I was pleased to think that, in some small way, we'd brought it back around to this place.

The cemetery was a different story. The kids were getting restless and starting to fuss, but luckily, we soon found the Hobson plot with its large monument and yew hedges. Both boys charged out of the car and into the light rain, laughing and running around on top of their dead ancestors, including William, Frank, and Dora Hobson. While Steph tried to contain them, I searched for Clifford's marker. I finally found it around the back side of the hedges, set off to the side and partially hidden by a large tree. The roots had pushed up a corner of the small flat stone. There was a woman's headstone next to his, which at first I thought might be a second wife, but Norma's chart confirmed it was his sister.

So this is how it ends for failed fathers and husbands, I thought. *Sleeping for eternity next to your sister.*

It was a fate I hoped to avoid, and was convinced I would. We may have looked similar, Clifford and I, but like homographic words, I was sure our lives wouldn't ultimately mean the same. Despite my stressed-out ways, I loved my wife and children, was totally committed to them, and could never imagine abandoning them.

"C'mere, Dad!" Ben shouted, crouching behind the giant Hobson monument. "A trap-door spider lair!"

Not again with the trap-door spider, I thought. *Can't anyone see I'm trying to have a private moment here?*

I walked over and saw there was indeed a small webbed tunnel extending beneath the stone. For no good reason, I told him it probably wasn't the work of a trap-door spider, but Ben was oblivious to my efforts to douse his enthusiasm. He still insisted it *was* a trap-door spider, and directed us to search the grass for a webby bag full of insect parts, which it had probably tried to pull over the hole when it heard us coming.

"Spiders do crazy things when they're afraid," he said.

"Yes," I replied. "So do people. Now it's time to get ready to go."

Ben whined as Steph gently escorted the boys back to the car— "I think it was a trap-door spider," I heard her tell him. I returned to Clifford's grave, hoping for one last quiet moment. As I reflected on his life, I certainly didn't see any connection between his choices as a father and my own. What I had yet to appreciate, however, was that there are many forms of fatherly abandonment. How many times in the years before and after that moment had I used my own needs and preoccupations, big and small, as an excuse to chase away my family? How many times had fear—fear of failure, of "squandered" time, of losing control—caused me to retreat inside my own internal lair?

If those impulses were allowed to grow, unchecked, what would be the consequences for my family, my children? What final loneliness might the future hold for me?

Be a good father. Not like mine.

Blood will tell.

These were just words, yet to be spoken or read, but I think they already existed inside my body, inside the tangibles and intangibles that had led to my creation. They had become flesh, and I'd carried them with me, like Clifford's face, all the way back to his grave.

As perhaps he knew I would.

7

Baby vs. Pengy!

WHILE CONTEMPLATING Clifford Hobson's failures, I'd often put myself in his parents' place as they lay in bed at night, thinking about the ways their son "did not take responsibility," the granddaughters and great-granddaughters they would never really know, and the regret over not steering their son in a different direction when they'd had the chance. And on the other side, the anger and resentment of parents whose daughter and granddaughters had been betrayed and abandoned by that irresponsible boy, publicly humiliated (Lehigh was a small town), and left to others to support. My grandmother had inherited a good portion of that anger, refusing to relinquish it, even though it had done her and her family nothing but harm, and there was no chance of reparations or justice. Here, perhaps, was an example of bad karma at work, the consequences of one person's actions rippling out across the generations, across the lives of countless other people, poisoning their hearts.

It was almost enough to make one not want to be a parent—I mean, who needs the pressure?

Since that bus had already departed, I was left to consider how this unfortunate family legacy might be turned around. Despite my own imperfections, how might I teach my children to deal with responsibility and disappointment and anger in a healthier way? Especially in relation to those they love?

Recently, when a bitter feud erupted between Spencer and another boy in the neighborhood, just such a teachable moment appeared to present itself. The dispute involved two stuffed toys and a woolly bear caterpillar—a fact that, you might assume, would have lowered the intensity. On the contrary, the imaginary status of the combatants only seemed to increase the emotional stakes for everyone involved. This was partly our fault. When it came to imaginary friends, Steph and I had always been a little overindulgent. When Ben was one year old his Grandma Sondra gave him a Woody the Cowboy doll, from the *Toy Story* movies he loved to watch. He carried that doll with him everywhere, talking and playing with him, even feeding him, until Woody was almost unrecognizable beneath the accumulated grime. At one point, Woody's much-loved head nearly fell off. Steph set up a surgical hospital in the living room and, with a worried Ben looking on, carefully sewed it back onto his neck. Woody was then transported to the intensive care unit, otherwise known as our couch, where for almost a week Ben attended to his every need. During the recovery period, no one was allowed to sit on the couch for fear of disturbing the ailing cowpoke. If someone accidentally sat there, such as a distracted father hoping to catch a portion of the evening news, Ben would erupt:

"Daddy sit on floor!"

And with surprisingly little complaint, Daddy would obey.

Ben eventually moved on to flesh-and-blood friends, but then it was Spencer's turn. Since he was a toddler, Spencer had been playing "Daddy" to a small doll he called "Baby." Baby was about eight inches long with a stuffed, white fabric torso, royal blue velvet jumpsuit, and plastic limbs that flopped around unnaturally. His big plastic head could bend completely backward, allowing him to stare at you upside down with his glassy eyes. Frankly, I found him a little spooky. He combined two of my worst childhood horrors—animated dolls and, when Spencer dressed Baby in his little striped nightcap, clowns. Even without the subconscious associations, something just wasn't right about that doll. Underneath the cherub face, the dimpled grin, I sensed darker forces at play.

I wasn't alone. Sometimes, out of misplaced affection, Spencer would sneak Baby into Ben's top bunk after he'd fallen asleep. Ben would awake in the morning to find the doll lying next to his head, giving him that upside down stare, and scream.

Spencer, though, had a way of gifting his love to those who most needed it, and there was no doubt: this scary mini desperately needed it. Baby returned that love, becoming Spencer's constant companion and confidant. He joined his "Daddy Spencer" for birthday parties, backyard adventures, car trips, sleepovers in our bed, and occasionally baths, after which he was required to take a "fun" ride in the dryer. One time Steph left him in too long (accident?) and his plastic scalp began to melt and smoke. His blue eyes turned purple. Spencer, distraught, smothered Baby's entire head with bacitracin and wrapped it in toilet paper, which reminded me of that Tennyson poem about doomed soldiers in the Crimean War: *Theirs but to do and die.* It's a line that could be applied to many of our toys.

After the dryer incident, we had no choice but to officially adopt Baby as one of the family. He enjoyed full privileges, including his own chair at the dinner table, a spot in all the family photos, and even his own baby-sized stocking for Santa to fill on Christmas Eve. I suppose he was our first unofficial grandchild.

In truth, the boys' inclination toward imaginary friends may have been an inherited genetic flaw. When I was around Ben's age or even a little older—too old, really—I became emotionally attached to a green plastic elf boy known from the Jolly Green Giant television commercials as "Lil' Sprout." My grandpa Roy was the district manager of Safeway grocery stores, and he would often pass along fun promotional items, such as a cigarette lighter that played the jingle for Butternut Bread and an eight-inch jackknife with "Dole Banana" inscribed in blood red on the handle. What fire or razor-sharp jackknives had to do with either product was beyond me, but I happily accepted these items and many others.

Lil' Sprout, however, took hold of my heart. There was just something about the big green eyes, the leafy hair and tunic, and the bean stem growing out of his crown that said, *Love me!* I carried him everywhere, bestowing on him the gifts of speech and intelligence and the power to ward off all brands of evil—including the green vegetables his Jolly Green father, with the help of my mother, regularly tried to force on me.

Unfortunately, our Brittany spaniel, Chrissy, also developed an affection for Lil' Sprout. I caught her chewing on him a number of times before he disappeared altogether, leaving me distraught. His body would be found over a decade later in the dirt where Chrissy's doghouse had once been. He cleaned up surprisingly well and was currently perched on a bookshelf in my study, where the boys sometimes played with him. The first few weeks after his disappearance, however, I was inconsolable, and it was a long time before I risked another serious relationship with an inanimate object. Eventually, in late elementary school, I became attached to a series of plastic Hallmark holiday pins—a Halloween owl, an Easter chick popping out of an egg, a leprechaun, a turkey, a Santa Claus that played "Jingle Bells" when you pressed his nose. I was already unpopular, and wearing these pins to school did nothing to improve that status. I didn't care. I wanted the other kids to believe I'd absorbed the powers of these magical friends, but what those powers were I could only guess—and so could they, loudly.

"Jingle bells, John Price smells!"

Memories of that public humiliation created perhaps some unwarranted anxiety about Spencer's increasing obsession with Baby—would he outgrow it sooner than I did? More important, what was that imaginary relationship teaching him about the real world? How would it influence Spencer's relationships with friends—or even a future spouse and children—who could actually talk back and hold opinions? Creatures who had their own needs and desires outside of his own? If responding to those needs became too inconvenient, would he simply abandon his responsibilities like Clifford Hobson did? Or retreat internally, like his father sometimes did? Or would he be one of those individuals who skips human intimacy altogether, moves into a basement, and falls in love with a blow-up doll?

Thankfully, we weren't the only parents in the neighborhood facing the challenge. William, the five-year-old across the street, had been in a long-term relationship with a small, juvenile penguin named "Pengy." Pengy was made of stuffed cloth and felt, with a soft orange beak and black marble eyes. Like Baby, he had earned real-life privileges and affection from his human family. Penguin books and movies and coloring books filled the shelves in William's bedroom. William had studied them all, becoming the neighborhood's resident polar ornithologist, able to rattle off all sorts of penguin facts. For Christmas, his father had even purchased a lighted penguin that stood in the front yard and flapped its wings.

It got a little weird at times for Steph and me and William's parents, carrying on extended conversations with Baby and Pengy, occasionally at the same time. But despite that weirdness and other worries, none of us was willing to risk stomping on our children's imaginations.

Until it was too late.

Baby and Pengy were good friends at first, and actually had a lot to teach each other—and us. We learned, for example, that the needs of human babies and juvenile penguins are surprisingly similar. Both require a lot of parental protection when they are young, except that in the case of penguins, the dads mostly take care of the babies while the moms march off to find food. If the moms don't return, the babies die. William frequently reminded us of this horrifying fact, as did Ben and Spencer, perhaps because it was an all-too-realistic scenario. How many times, when Steph had been unexpectedly late returning from errands, had the boys approached me with pensive looks:

"When's Momma getting back?"

They understood, as did I, that without her we'd soon perish from starvation and neglect.

Baby, for his part, was a blossoming entomologist and led Pengy and the neighborhood children on many insect-spotting expeditions. They especially liked to explore the woods in the neighboring yard, and the owners, Bob and Elaine, were kind enough to let them do it. Their own daughter, Krista, became an ecology professor, so that stretch of woods had a reputation for encouraging young naturalists. After a few hours, our children usually emerged from the trees with all sorts of interesting arti-facts. Trading would ensue: an old license plate for a handful of cicada husks, an antique glass inkwell for a red-tailed hawk feather, two silver rings for a possum's skull. It was a win-win situation—the kids learned about nature and, along the way, picked up the litter.

Then a woman came between them. A female woolly bear cat-erpillar to be precise. I didn't actually know its gender, but Spen-cer had declared it a "her," and we obliged. "Woolly" was a looker, no doubt about it—with soft, fully-fluffed brown fur and sporting a lovely burnt sienna stole—destined to spark jealousy wherever she crawled. When Spencer and Baby first discovered her, she didn't crawl at all. She appeared to be dead, curled into a rigid ball, but Spencer wasn't ready to give up. He carried her around with him for the better part of two days, during which she suddenly revived—more proof, Ben insisted, that death has no dominion.

Spencer enthusiastically welcomed Woolly into his imaginary family. Often he would place the caterpillar on Baby's head and let it crawl around on his face and body, which, for the rest of us, only amplified the doll's creepiness. Woolly rarely attempted to detach herself from his bald scalp—probably because she was hanging on for dear life, as Spencer took them everywhere. At night, he would put Woolly in Brownie's old peanut butter jar with some fresh twigs and grass. He'd set it next to his bottom bunk, where Baby could watch her until he slipped into plastic dreamland.

One afternoon, while a shirtless Spencer was taking Baby and Woolly for a walk in the woods, he was joined by Ben and William and Pengy. According to Ben, the trouble began when William claimed Pengy was crying because he didn't have his own woolly bear friend. Feeling sorry for the young bird, Baby allowed Pengy to carry Woolly on his cloth flipper, but only for a few minutes. At some point during that short period of time, the caterpillar disappeared. There were multiple accounts of what happened next, but according to Ben, Spencer became unhinged, screaming and essentially accusing Pengy of negligent homicide. Spencer then picked up a rock and chased Pengy (and William) back to their house across the street, where William slammed and locked the door.

Spencer returned home sobbing and hugging Baby, who, he claimed, "is very, very mad and wants to hurt Pengy." We had a long talk with Spencer about how "accidents happen," and how Woolly would be just fine in her natural environment. We also scolded him for attempting to throw a rock at Pengy, emphasizing how he might have accidentally hurt William. This was perhaps the opportunity I'd been looking for to teach our children about controlling their impulses and being willing to let go of anger and the need for revenge. The fact that I—and several other ancestors—had trouble letting go of these emotions didn't seem worth mentioning, though Spencer, like most kids, could smell hypocrisy a mile off. He eyed me suspiciously. Ben tried to do his part by informing Spencer that if he were to actually hit William with a rock, he would end up in "juvie," where they "make you drink Gatorade that's actually someone's pee."

That seemed to do the trick. Spencer promised he wouldn't hurt Pengy, or anyone else, and we all hugged.

Baby, however, wasn't quite ready to make nice.

It began when Pengy mysteriously disappeared during outdoor playtime, only to be spotted in the upper branches of one of the pear trees. As I retrieved him with the pruning pole, everyone watched—everyone except Baby, who sat at the base of the tree with his back to us. The next day, Pengy was discovered floating facedown in the birdbath, while Baby relaxed on a nearby deck chair. A few days after that, when William came over to play with Ben, Steph found Pengy buried neck deep in the litter box.

After this last incident, which required giving Pengy a time-consuming sponge bath in the sink, we had a private chat with Spencer. To each of our pointed inquiries, Spencer's response was the same:

"Accidents happen."

The conflict divided the children of the neighborhood, pitting friend against friend, brother against brother. Zach, Hannah, and William's younger twin siblings, Gabriel and Stevie, were on the side of Baby—Pengy *should* have been more careful, they said. Ben, Gracie, and Emma thought the young bird shouldn't be punished for accidentally losing Woolly. Emma had lost a hamster herself and no one had thrown a rock at her head.

I was of two minds about the issue. Seen from one angle, Spencer was a boy losing his temper in inappropriate ways, and then trying to avoid accountability. Seen from another, he was like the young naturalist Edward Abbey when he proclaimed personal responsibility for all the creatures in Arches National Park: "It is my duty as a park ranger to protect, preserve and defend all living things within the park boundaries, making no exceptions. . . . I prefer not to kill animals. I'm a humanist; I'd rather kill a *man* than a snake."

Spencer appeared to have taken the same oath, but took it even further, making no distinction between family and nature. From his perspective, when it came to caring for the planet and those who reside here, especially the small and vulnerable—whether animals and insects, or your own children—there were no "accidents." There was only sacred duty.

As a fellow parent, I could understand where Spencer was coming from. Steph and I had been a bit overprotective ourselves at times—especially of Spencer. That may have had something to do with the fact that he was born with ptosis, a condition where the muscles in the eyelids don't fully develop, causing them to droop. Ptosis is a localized form of muscular dystrophy, though I doubted Jerry would be inviting us to the Vegas telethon. Spencer just had a droopy left eyelid, which we affectionately called "The Winky." That affection didn't stop people, including complete strangers, from commenting on it or singlehandedly trying to correct it. Once, while in line at the grocery store, a man reached out and physically lifted my son's eyelid. I was tempted to do the same to him, with my fist.

The ptosis hadn't yet affected Spencer's eyesight, the main risk, but doctors still recommended preemptive surgery. Steph and I struggled with the decision. We'd grown attached to The Winky, for one—it was a unique part of Spencer, the boy we loved. Then there were the possible side effects of the surgery, including scarring and the inability to fully close the eyelid during sleep, like certain reptiles and fish. On the other hand, Spencer had begun commenting on his eyelid in photographs and in the mirror, even trying to lift it up a couple of times himself. He once asked Steph and me what was "wrong" with his eye, and we told him nothing was wrong with it. It was beautiful.

"Caitlyn says it's freaky," he replied, and again I felt the anger rise within me. *Who was this Caitlyn? What kind of parents would raise such a cruel little monster? Where's a rock?!*

The parallels between my own occasionally overprotective, judgmental impulses as a parent and Spencer's relationship to

Baby and Woolly were clear. But was that a good thing? Despite my earlier worries about imaginary friends, I was proud Spencer felt so responsible for those in his care, whether alive or stuffed. The fact that a boy was willing to go to such extremes to love and protect a caterpillar made it seem even more unnatural that a man, a father, wouldn't do the same for his own children. It was also clear, however, that this responsibility could be taken too far, clouding judgment and causing even more suffering.

Or was that just another cop-out?

I didn't know. Maybe that's why, when it came to the battle between Baby and Pengy, I eventually elected to behave like the Japanese bystanders in a *Godzilla* movie and do my best to get out of the way. No doubt the conflict would soon run its course, and everything would return to normal. Steph agreed and confessed she hadn't been as disturbed to find Pengy in the litter box as perhaps she should've been. We laughed about it all and began to relax.

That was our mistake. A few days later, William and Ben and Pengy were playing cars near the garage when, suddenly, there was a shriek. The boys looked up to see Baby hurtling over the deck railing, directly toward them. What William thought as that creepy doll descended through the air toward his face, God only knows. The boy must have frozen from terror, because Baby nailed him square in the forehead. The result for William was a small welt and lots of tears and a forced apology from Spencer. The result for Baby was solitary confinement on the top shelf of the kitchen cupboard.

Spencer was outraged. We appreciated the sensitive nature of the case, and could see things from his point of view—Pengy had betrayed Baby's trust by carelessly losing his loved one in the woods, leaving her vulnerable to predators and all sorts of other dangers. That was wrong, no doubt about it. Still, Spencer needed to understand there were consequences for his own hurtful, vengeful behavior. Once he started down that path, where would it end? Spencer nonetheless continued to loudly protest Baby's incarceration, claiming he'd been playing with the doll on the deck, when it just "slipped out" of his hands and flew over the railing.

"Baby didn't mean to hit William!" he cried.

Technically, this may have been true—Pengy was most likely the primary target, and William just collateral damage. We nonetheless insisted the doll take an extended time-out. Spencer pleaded that Baby wouldn't survive hard time in the kitchen cupboard. It was too dark and dusty up there, he cried, and there were mice—Baby was terrified of mice. He probably knew this last argument would carry some additional weight with his parents, and indeed, a plea deal was soon reached. In exchange for better accommodations, Baby pled guilty to the lesser charge of "not being careful while playing on the deck." Baby was put under supervised house arrest for a week, followed by extended probation. If he so much as smiled at Pengy, even an upside down smile, it would be back to the cupboard.

A few days later, Steph bolted into the kitchen and announced that Woolly had been found—*alive*! We all rushed over to see the caterpillar crawling along Steph's knuckles. She said she found her on the mulberry stump in the backyard, near the woods. Spencer hesitated a moment, and I was afraid he'd noticed that this Woolly was a little smaller, her sienna stole thinner, her fur not quite as fluffy. Then there was the fact that Woolly had originally disappeared deep in the woods, and for her to make it back to the top of the mulberry stump would've been the human equivalent of traversing the Amazonian rain forest on foot, then climbing Devils Tower.

I could see Spencer weighing that improbability against his own desire that this be the same Woolly he had loved and thought lost. The result of that inner battle was predictable.

Spencer held out his hand, and Woolly crawled on over.

During the weeks ahead, the neighborhood children became friends again and all seemed forgotten. But feelings of anger and betrayal don't vanish that easily, as Grandma K could have reminded us. They can live on, across the generations, across the boundaries between one being and another, alive or dead. From time to time, I would still have to retrieve Pengy from the top of the pear tree or from the thorny blackberry bramble or from under one of the cars, waiting to be run over.

"An accident," I would be told, again and again, and I would almost believe it.

But then, somewhere nearby, I would spot a pair of purple glass eyes staring at me, defying me to claim that his cause, by any other name, wasn't justice.

8

Providerection

MY PARENTS INVITED Ben and Spencer to spend a few days with them and Grandma K in Fort Dodge, so I drove the kids to meet them halfway in the small town of Denison. My father had spent a good portion of his childhood in Denison, where his father, Roy, had managed the Safeway store before being transferred to Fort Dodge. Grandpa Roy always maintained a soft spot for Denison, which, he often reminded us, was the hometown of Donna Reed, star of *It's a Wonderful Life*—a distinction we kids didn't fully appreciate. Grandpa never met Donna in person, he was sorry to say, but her folks had been loyal customers of Safeway's meat department. He was certain the starlet had consumed more than a few pounds of his Grade-A Prime during her visits from Hollywood.

The boys were thrilled to see their grandparents, and they waved to me from the backseat of their car as they headed off to

Fort Dodge. I waved and blew kisses, but secretly couldn't wait to be free of the noisy distraction of kids for a few days. I had plans to finish another novel chapter and also complete some long-neglected home repairs. My anxieties about our rundown house cranked into full gear as I drove past the town sign: "Denison: It's a Wonderful Life." Despite the sort of family connection to Donna Reed, the first time I'd actually watched that film all the way through was during a frigid evening the previous December. I'd been channel surfing, shivering under two sweaters and a blanket, because the house had virtually no insulation, when I stumbled upon the opening credits. I thought I might as well watch a few minutes, just to take my mind off the frostbite. I soon became completely entranced, and remained so until the final credits rolled into darkness. It wasn't so much the human drama that got me, though I felt in my cold bones all of George's conflicted emotions about staying home, his ineffectual response to stress, and his frustrated desire to travel the world. My international experience had been limited to a family reunion in Victoria, Canada, and a couple of shopping trips with Grandma K to the border town of Nogales, Mexico, when she was living in Arizona. Not exactly the Grand Tour.

No, what really gripped me was George's piece-of-crap house. I was moved beyond expression by the young James Stewart and Donna Reed making wishes and throwing rocks through the windows of that old abandoned structure. Even more moved by the fact that they undoubtedly had to repair those same windows when they bought the place as a married couple. I would have loved to hear that conversation. Then there was the banister knob, which kept coming off in George's hand. For me, it was the spiritual heart of the film, and it was a dark one. It seemed obvious that it wasn't the lost bank deposit that ultimately drove George over the edge, but that stupid banister knob and all the accumulating frustrations associated with their "romantic" old mansion. George, in fact, decided to kill himself shortly after barking at his daughter for banging on the piano—who but an owner of an old house understood how plaster-and-lath walls amplify noise beyond bearable levels?

And the pile of money his friends and family gave him at the end? After he paid off the bank, I knew exactly where that was going. Plumbing.

From my point of view, George's relationship to his house infected everything in his life, including his relationship with his father. The focus there appeared to be on Mr. Bailey's attempt to guilt his son into taking over the family business, but the real source of dramatic tension, as I experienced it, was his failure to teach George any fix-it skills. I had a similar father, a good and ethical man, dedicated to the well-being of others in his community, but one who had failed to pass on any home repair knowledge to his offspring. My earliest memory of Dad's effort to renovate the Kelley house involved a pen and a checkbook. Only last year, he'd confessed to taking a half day to change the furnace filter. Mom claimed he used to do the mowing, but had handed that off to me shortly after I learned to walk. That was a tradition I hoped to continue with my boys, though I planned to wait until they were at least nine. In fairness, his father, Grandpa Roy, hadn't been much of a fix-it guy either, having lived in an apartment all the years I'd known him—an option that was looking more attractive every day.

In the meantime, I'd sworn to learn the necessary home improvement skills, so I might bequeath my sons the masculine birthright I had been denied.

That effort had been mixed. When we first moved in, I took on the seemingly simple task of painting the ten-foot walls in the living room, which the previous owners had painted robin egg blue, including the wood trim and fireplace. I also stripped and painted the dining room walls, which had been covered with purple and pink striped wallpaper, most likely to hide the massive cracks. This effort cost me three weeks and innumerable brain cells from the chemical fumes. Once the painting was finished, I couldn't wait to hang the first framed picture. After locating the perfect spot, I carefully centered the nail, but when I tapped the hammer, the plaster exploded as if I'd unloaded a shotgun into it. There were numerous other "teaching moments," such as when I used one of those compressed-air drain cleaners to unclog our bathroom sink. When I dispensed the canister into the drain, the force shot a century's worth of filth back into my face and detached the pipe from the wall.

Apparently I hadn't been the only resident to view the place as a giant shop class. Steph and I referred to these previous do-it-yourselfers, collectively, as "Mr. F"—which stood for "Mr. Fix-It" or, depending on the situation, "Mr. Fuck-Up." It was the latter Mr. F who had, for example, sealed plumbing pipes with cement and removed all the beautiful interior oak doors, painted them sea-green, and used them as walls for his basement darkroom. The same Mr. F had been inspired, in 1920, to use an acetylene torch to remove exterior paint, burning half the house down. The rebuilt structure we lived in retained many of the original Victorian details on the ground floor, but walk upstairs and you found yourself in an Arts and Crafts bungalow. The place was an architectural Frankenstein.

Now, with me on board, the house had a whole new reason to be paranoid.

But there were other threats of the nonhuman variety. Enter the ants. We'd suffered pest invasions before, such as mice and hordes of Asian lady beetles (known to the boys as "ladybugs"), but these devils took it to a whole new level. The spring after Spencer was born, Steph noticed an unusual number of black ants in the kitchen, but neither of us gave it much thought. Then, one morning, I was consuming a syrup-drenched pile of French toast when Ben pointed at the Mrs. Butterworth's bottle.

"What's that in the bottom?" he asked.

Closer inspection revealed "that" to be a thick sludge of dead ants—hundreds of them! At some point, they'd crawled in the open nozzle and drowned.

Ben giggled, mostly because, unlike me, he'd opted for powdered sugar instead of syrup on his French toast. Steph giggled too, but then the front deck collapsed and the ants weren't so funny anymore.

The guy we hired to repair it took his sweet time clearing out and replacing the ant-decimated wood. I'd sometimes find him sitting on the steps, admiring the wildflowers in our front garden.

"Amazing what God has made for this world, isn't it?"

"Yes," I wanted to say, "but we shouldn't plan on Him fixing the deck."

He eventually finished the job, but the time and cost made me feel even more inadequate. As did the continued presence of the ants. I was ready to call the exterminator, but Steph didn't want the kids breathing the pesticide or touching the residue. She researched some nontoxic solutions, which as usual involved more work, but they seemed to do the trick. For a while.

This spring, the ants had returned in force. In the cupboards and under the sink, as before, but now expanding their range to include the upstairs bedrooms. The other morning I was awakened by one of them crawling into my mouth. I'd just about consumed my fill of ants by that time, but even more disturbing was the thought of what they were undoubtedly doing inside the walls of our house and to our deck. If the deck collapsed again, I still wouldn't be able to repair it, and was even less prepared to pay someone else to do the job.

On the drive back from Denison, one thought led to another until I was overwhelmed not just by anxiety over the ants but also over the rotting trim around the windows, the peeling paint on the garage, the leaky gutters, the dripping faucets, the cracks in the plaster walls, and the host of other minor disasters needing my attention. In truth, the entire house probably needed an overhaul—foundation, walls, roof, windows, insulation, basement, the whole damn thing.

Maybe it was time for another go with the acetylene torch.

As I walked up the creaky steps to our front door, I thought of George Bailey leaning over the edge of that bridge. I wasn't to that point yet, but what was wrong with a little preemptive divine intervention? Why couldn't God send me an angel right now, and preferably one with a tool bag?

Then, as if on cue, I spotted an ant crawling along one of the boards on the deck. After the initial rage, I reminded myself that I'd manhandled these suckers before and I could do it again. During the last scourge, I'd spread diatomaceous earth around the foundation of the house, which is made of the fossilized remains of diatoms, a type of hard-shelled algae. As ants and spiders and other insects crawl through, the substance cuts into their exoskeletons and they die of dehydration. When I told Steph my diabolical plan, she reminded me of the No-Kill Law and Ben's love of spiders. The only humane option, she said, was to mix up another batch of her special "ant discourager," a heady brew of mostly peppermint oil, mixed with crushed mint leaves, cloves, cinnamon, lemon juice, and cayenne pepper. Spreading this stuff around the interior of the house, on my hands and knees, sneezing all the way, was not something I looked forward to. I knew from experience that despite wearing gloves, it would get into the pores of my skin, as well my hair and nose follicles (at least those that didn't disintegrate), and stay there for days.

"Do you want me to help?" Steph asked. I could tell the offer wasn't entirely sincere.

"No, I'll do it myself."

I purchased the ingredients, mixed them in a saucepan, and using the tip of a dishrag, spread it along the baseboards of every room in the house, the kitchen cabinets, and the door and window frames. I then moved outside and, after sprinkling chopped garlic between the deck boards (I'd read somewhere that this helps), spread more ant discourager along the perimeter of the deck and also the foundation. After the initial drag, the whole process took on a momentum of its own, an almost ritual-like rhythm in which I lost myself for a while. Or maybe that was the fumes.

By the time I finished, I was feeling pretty good about myself and my guilt-free, No-Kill effort to protect my family from a potentially hazardous insect invasion. No one need fear walking on the deck or eating French toast again—at least for another year.

"Looks like someone has a providerection," Steph commented as I sauntered into the kitchen. Providerection is her term for what a man experiences when he thinks he's successfully provided for or protected his family, and I guess I was feeling it. She came over to give me a hug.

"You may not want to do that," I warned. "I reek."

"Nonsense," she said, as she put her arms around my neck. "I like my man to smell like candy cane and gumbo."

It was a moment, among many, when I felt intensely the happiness of being married.

Just after supper, I thought I'd finally take advantage of the absence of kids and do a little writing at the dining room table, where I could spread out my drafts. It didn't take long, however, to be distracted by another domestic responsibility. On the nearby library table was Spencer's terrarium. Following the "return" of Woolly the caterpillar, Spencer had become obsessed with her well-being, so he and his mother (and Baby) had turned an old fishbowl into a miniature of our backyard, complete with dirt and rocks and treelike plants. A piece of perforated tin foil rested on top. Spencer added his own personal touches, such as plastic dinosaurs, seashells, and a giant peacock feather that rose two feet out of the center. Its blue-green eye kept watch over the tiny world, like the Masonic Eye of God.

"The International Woolly Bear Preserve," we called it.

But a peacock feather could only be trusted so far, and before Spencer and Baby left for Fort Dodge, they'd made me promise to check on Woolly. I couldn't spot the caterpillar from my seat at the dining room table, and remembering what happened the last time we lost her, I got up to have a closer look. She was hard to locate in the now dense, living jungle of the preserve, but I eventually spotted her climbing on a twig. I also noticed she had a number of new friends, including several roly-polies, a couple of modest-sized crickets, and a katydid.

Spencer clearly wasn't intimidated by his responsibility to meet the needs of a growing family, which included providing them with a suitable, even beautiful habitat. Why should I be?

An hour or so later, the phone rang, and Steph told me it was the boys. They wanted to talk to me.

"Hi, Dad," Ben said. "Today we went on a picnic with Grandpa and Grandma and Gramma K, and guess what?"

"What?"

"Gramma K says she's going to die pretty soon. Here's Spencer."

"Wait. . . ."

"Daddy, I'm sad," Spencer's quiet voice spoke into the phone. "Why does Gramma K have to die? Why doesn't she take her medicine, like she's supposed to?"

"I don't know, Spencer. I guess, well. . . ." There was a pause as I tried to find the right words.

"Bye, Daddy," he finally said, and hung up.

I called back and my sister Carrie answered the phone. She was visiting Fort Dodge with her oldest daughter, Abigail, who was eight. I asked her what happened on the picnic. She said they were all at Dolliver State Park, where the kids had just finished playing in the creek, splashing and chasing minnows. They were sitting at the picnic table when, in the middle of passing around the fried chicken and potato salad, Grandma K suddenly announced she was getting ready to die. She didn't put it exactly like that, Carrie said, but it was close. This prompted a barrage of questions from the kids about when she was going to die and how and why, which she did her best to answer, but apparently not to the satisfaction of Spencer, who began crying and had to be distracted by a return trip to the creek.

"Did she honestly think a picnic was the best time to tell them about this?" I asked.

"Apparently, and now we all have to deal with the aftermath."

After we hung up, I went outside and slumped into the deck

chair. Spencer had wanted answers, or just a few reassuring words, and I'd failed to provide him with any. Now he and Ben were beyond reach, alone with their thoughts and worries as dusk—this same dusk—was falling.

All that I'd accomplished that day, or in my life as a father, felt meaningless.

The smell of garlic was overwhelming, and I was preparing to go inside when a wood roach crawled up between the deck boards and paused near my shoe. I could see its brethren darting around in other places. These are the outdoor, "country cousins" of the common variety found in homes. In my obsession with the ants, I'd forgotten all about the roaches and their annoying habit of skittering over our bare feet and ankles whenever we were caught lounging on the deck at sundown.

What could be done? Resistant to nuclear radiation, there was little chance these prehistoric pests would be repelled by peppermint oil and garlic. As a species, they probably would outlive us all.

Not this one, I thought, and stepped on it.

A couple of days after getting the call from Ben and Spencer, I drove to Fort Dodge to pick them up. I'd told Steph to stay home and enjoy a few more days of peace and quiet. I truly wanted her to have a break from all of us—God knows she'd earned it—but I think I also wanted the chance to make up for my earlier failure to comfort the boys. The writing and house repairs weren't progressing anyway, so I might as well try to fix something else. Something that mattered.

When I pulled into my parents' driveway in Fort Dodge, I was greeted by screams emanating from the house. I thought of the bad karma created by that squashed roach—had yet another murder been committed? Spencer and Abby burst out of the door and ran toward the car.

"What's happened?" I asked, the panic rising.

"Ben has a tick!" Spencer sputtered. "Ben has a tick!"

"Gramma's getting it off!" Abby added. "Hurry and see!"

When the kids pulled me into the kitchen, I saw my mother poised over Ben's head with some tweezers, cackling like a witch, which she did whenever she was nervous.

"Now that's enough screaming Ben, *hee-hee-hee,* this will only take a second, *hee-hee-hee.*"

"Daddy!" Ben cried when he saw me, reaching out his arms. "Gramma's gone crazy! She's going to pinch me!"

"Just look at this tick, John," she said, trying to control herself.

I saw that there was indeed a tick attached to his scalp, while Spencer and Abby got up close for another peek at the monster. Ticks were the insecto-terrorists of the Iowa child's summer, sneaking their way into otherwise happy outdoor excursions to dispense fear and disease. When we were kids, it had been standard procedure to "burn" the tick off with a smoking hot match, while we squirmed and screamed out of fear our parents would set our hair on fire. It turned out we were right about the danger. The hot match removed the tick, but only after causing it to dispense even more saliva into the wound.

Although it was too late for me—who knew what diseases I'd been carrying around since childhood—I was relieved to see Mom had replaced the smoking match with the more conventional (and safer) tweezers. The screaming child was the same, however.

"Don't let her pinch me, Daddy!"

"Grandma's right, Ben, it has to come off. Don't worry, it won't hurt . . . much."

She gently grabbed the tick with the tweezers and, with one last cackle, pulled it off.

"Is it over?" Ben asked, eyes shut tight. Mom held up the nasty thing for him and the rest of the kids to admire. When Spencer suggested she put it in a jar and keep it as a pet, she paused.

"Sure, and why don't we give it a little bath as well." She placed it in a mason jar, then added a splash of rubbing alcohol. The tick squirmed for a bit, then stopped.

"Look how much he enjoys that," she said. "Now we'll put it

on Grandpa's study desk, so he can enjoy it when he comes home from work. Anyone want to go to the park?"

I felt like taking notes.

That evening, after Carrie and Abby had left for home, Grandma called and said she wanted me to come over. The boys were finishing up dinner, but Mom said she'd drive them out later for their nightly swim at Friendship Haven, which had become a tradition.

When I entered her apartment, Grandma was placing a favorite record of church hymns on the turntable, while Niña tore around the room, barking and nipping at my shoelaces. Grandma invited me to sit down on the couch with her, and Niña jumped up and claimed the space between us.

"So how's work going?" she asked.

"Not so great."

"Well, at least you're doing what you love. I still don't understand why you gave up medicine—if you could be a doctor, why wouldn't you be? Most of the men I knew in the Depression didn't have that choice."

Here we go again, I thought. Grandma had often talked about how Grandpa Andy could have been this, could have been that, if only the Depression hadn't forced him to give up his plans for college and support his aging parents, and then his wife and daughter. She was right, to a point. During the Depression, an entire generation of fathers had to find work where they could, not where they wanted. Stephanie's grandfather Lloyd, in order to support his family, had worked as a gas station mechanic in rural Missouri, a cigar roller and paint color mixer in Kansas City, a gold miner in Cripple Creek, Colorado, and finally as an electrician for a paper mill in Tama, Iowa. All of it self-trained.

Choosing a profession was a luxury many of these men never enjoyed. To not use that choice to improve your social and economic standing, as I had apparently failed to do, came perilously close to sin.

"Don't worry," she continued, perhaps noticing my discomfort,

"I'm still proud of you. In fact, I was just showing off your book to some friends of mine who dropped by."

Grandma revealed that a lot of friends were dropping by, now that they knew the end was near. She wasn't complaining, she said, just stating a fact. Most just wanted to spend time with her or see if she needed anything. But some had other motivations.

"A group of my neighbors, including Verna across the hall, came by the other day to tell me they think I'm committing suicide and endangering my immortal soul. They're worried I'm going to hell. I hate to admit it, John, but I've begun to worry about it myself. Maybe I should call the whole thing off and take my medications again. What do you think?"

I could tell she was sincerely interested in my answer. My first impulse was to tell her Verna and her posse must be a pack of lunatics to say something like that to a dying person. But the truth of it was that I, too, had been hoping she'd call the whole thing off, albeit for different reasons. I simply didn't want her to die. From the moment she first announced her decision, part of me believed she would find a way out of it, that there would be time for her to change her mind, that there would be more time for her to spend with all of us, especially her great-grandchildren. I had to admit, though, that since going off the meds, she'd seemed mentally sharper and more physically comfortable. In whose interest would it be to tell her to give that up?

"I don't know what to say, Grandma. This is something you have to decide for yourself."

"Do you think this is suicide?"

"No, I don't. If anything, you're just letting nature take its course. You said the medicine made you sick and groggy, and that you didn't want to end things that way. I can't believe God would condemn you or anyone else for that."

She looked down at Niña, curled in her lap, while the church music continued to play in the background. It was one of her favorite hymns, "In the Garden."

And He walks with me, and He talks with me. He tells me I am His own. . . .

"Could you change that record?" she asked.

Not much later, Mom brought the boys over for their traditional nightly swim in "Gramma K's pool." They ran into her apartment, and after giving her a big hug, darted over to the dresser. Spencer pulled open the bottom drawer, and they grabbed a couple of Tootsie Rolls.

"I keep those there just for them," Grandma said. It was good to see her smile.

The Tootsie Rolls were part of a larger ritual they'd established together. After finishing their candy, the boys got a drink of water using what they called "Gramma's iceberg cups," which really did appear to be made of ice. Then they changed into their swimsuits, grabbed their towels, and it was off to the pool. Although it was only a short distance down the hall, the walk was prolonged by required stops at the parakeet cage, the popcorn machine, and the magazine pile in the library. Familiar neighbors waved at the boys and chatted with them, including Verna, the woman who'd told Grandma she was going to hell.

"Bye, Gramma Verna!" Ben called out as we moved on, and she blew him a kiss.

I asked Ben why he called her Gramma, and he said Verna had told them her grandchildren lived far away and hardly visited. Given what she'd said to my grandmother, I wasn't surprised. For Ben and Spencer, however, the only thing that mattered was that she was lonely. So the boys told her she could be their grandma too, but only if Gramma K said it was OK, which she did. That should have revealed to Verna more than enough information about the condition of her neighbor's soul.

Spencer hung on tightly to his great-grandmother's hand as we walked down the hall. He hadn't said anything more to me about her announcement at the park. Perhaps he'd given up on my ability to answer his questions. When we got to the pool, Spencer was reluctant to let go, but when he saw Ben jump in the water, he asked Grandma if it was OK to leave her. She said it was, and he allowed me to lead him to the shallow end.

Later that night, after tucking the kids into my childhood bed, I stepped downstairs to the study. I brought along my notebook, thinking I might do a little writing. The study was small but lined floor to ceiling with bookshelves. Growing up, I'd spent a lot of time perusing those shelves. Literature, art, history, religious philosophy, nature guides, family scrapbooks—it had all been there for me to pick up and sample. I didn't decide to become a writer until well into college, but I'm certain my parents' love of books, and their willingness to share them, set me on that path. Steph and I have tried to do the same with our children; there are always books scattered around the house to pick up or, occasionally, trip over.

An equally appealing feature of that study was the big picture window, looking out on a private spot with ferns and wildflowers and a giant spruce tree. Words, in that space, had gone hand-in-hand with natural beauty.

I turned on the desk lamp and opened my notebook, hoping the ambience of the study and the late hour would conjure some much-needed inspiration. I normally did my best writing late at night, when the kids were asleep and the day's preoccupations had long since closed shop. There was nowhere to go, nothing to do, not even anything decent to watch on TV. That was when the words usually came, which I considered precious, rare things. Too often, during the day, I became intent on forcing those words to appear, and then bending them to my will. At night, those expectations relaxed.

Recently, though, the daytime pressures had been regularly invading my nighttime sanctuary, as the "event" in March illustrated. This night was no different, as I thought of all the ways words had failed me during the last few days. With Spencer, with

Grandma. How I wished I could have offered them something more—more words, more wisdom. I was reminded of the narrator in Nabokov's *The Real Life of Sebastian Knight,* who "longs to say something real" to his brother after the death of their mother, "something with wings and a heart, but the birds I wanted settled on my shoulders and head only later when I was alone and not in need of words."

But here it was, later, and there were no birdlike words. Only moths, attracted by the desk lamp. Their skittering against the windowpane became a merciful distraction, the tiny noise that lets in the other noises of the night, the buzz of insects, the cricket songs, the hush of the breeze through the spruce. Their music made me unclench a little.

And that's when I saw the angel.

It appeared suddenly in the light of the window: huge, luminescent wings, flowing gown, and a pair of blinking eyes. Upon closer inspection, I realized it was a giant luna moth. As it moved in and out of the light, I almost couldn't believe it was real—the feathery antennae, the graceful, moon-green wings with their eye-like markings and long, curved tails. Since childhood, I'd considered lunas the holy grail of giant moths in Iowa, and had seen them only on the pages of books. Even there, they'd always appeared to be creatures from another realm. Elf queens or forest sprites or, yes, green angels.

When I was a boy, I sometimes would turn on my bedside lamp before going to sleep, hoping to attract a luna moth. I'd read that their larvae feed on walnut trees, and we had several of those in our yard. I'd also read that they mate, reproduce, and die within a few days. The adults never eat, never do any harm. They're just beautiful.

As I watched the moth, entranced, other childhood memories began to dance around the same light. I was transported to Dolliver State Park, where I'd spent so many days hiking and exploring. Grandma K had done the same thing in her youth. I'd questioned why she chose Dolliver as the place to tell Ben and

Spencer she was going to die, but maybe it had nothing to do with choice. I knew what would have surrounded them during that picnic this time of year. There would have been the sounds of clear-running Prairie Creek and its adjacent meadows full of color: the whites of rue anemone, the pinks of spring beauty. Beneath the bottom edges of the sandstone bluffs, the creek would have been tossing ripples of light against the shadows, while a hundred feet overhead, service berries would have been in full bloom, clinging to the high rock. A white petal or two would have fallen onto the water to float for a while, then vanish.

If they'd followed the main trail to the top of those bluffs, they would have come across two Indian mounds in a quiet meadow, speckled with waterleaf and Dutchman's breeches and, in the barely leafing branches, redheaded woodpeckers and flickers and maybe a sleepy owl or two. They might have continued on to the edge of the opposite bluff, with its view of the Des Moines River over a hundred feet below. The earth slopes so dramatically there they might have felt in danger of falling and reached out, as I always had, for the nearest tree trunk. Like me, they might have been afraid to let go, but also sort of wanted to.

I've returned many times to that place in my dreams, the steep bluff, the big river far below, the feeling that I will either fall or fly. I have done both.

Upstairs, my sons were inside their own dreams, but before they fell asleep, I wondered if they'd gazed out the same window I had as a boy, setting loose some of the same questions about life and death and the mysteries of nature. The questions with wings. After they fell asleep, did their dreams intersect with my own, my grandmother's, returning them to the magical world of Dolliver that linked all of our childhoods—the stream of minnows, the caves and cliff banks and burial mounds covered with blossoms?

Is that why she'd been moved to tell them out there? Was it a language they could understand? Did I understand it?

As I watched the luna moth, I considered how this creature, which I had so wanted to see as a child, had only found me now, when I was a grown-up father. Did it also carry with it the answer to all those childhood questions and dreams? If it did, I couldn't tell, for the choice between the two dreams, the two ways, seemed to have remained the same. To cling to the surface of your life, waiting, as I had on the deck with the ants and the roaches, for the world to collapse beneath you. Or to rise, like the luna, in an hour of fear to offer all the beauty you possess, to do no harm, to give everything for your family, your world, to accept what limited time you have, to not think of time at all.

To quit searching, even for words, even for that something with wings and a heart, and find joy in the wings themselves.

It was all right there, close enough to grasp, and I instinctively reached my hand toward the moth. My fingers touched the glass between us, and like that, it was gone.

9

Happy Goddamned International Ben Day!

ON FATHER'S DAY, Steph surprised me with breakfast in bed and a crying jag.

"You're the sweetest," I said as I hugged her, thinking the eggs and the tears had something to do with her deep appreciation for me as a husband and father.

"We have so much love to give, don't we?" she sniffled.

"Yes, we do," I replied.

"And we have such a great family, don't we? I mean, we've been so fortunate, right?"

"Yes, yes."

"And with a little help, don't you think you could turn the basement into a study?"

"Yes, of cour—" I pulled back. "What's this about?"

"John, I . . . I think we should have another *baby*. . . ."

She started sobbing again, which was convenient, since I was completely speechless. She'd mentioned the possibility of having another child before, but in a casual, almost joking way, so I hadn't taken it seriously. I mean, how could I? A few months after Spencer was born, following another brutal night of cluster nursing, Steph announced she didn't want any more babies, and that we could pack up and sell all the infant clothes and equipment after Spencer was done with them. Which is exactly what we did, holding a massive garage sale that netted us a whopping $51.51—I remember the depressing symmetry of it.

Now she was changing her mind? When we were both pushing forty?

I had a brief vision of the future: injuring my aging knee during a preschool round of Duck, Duck, Goose; or people exclaiming, during the child's various high-school events, how proud I must be of my "grandchild." By the time he or she was in college, I'd be on the verge of retirement, if I hadn't died already. Then again, life insurance might be the best option for covering the cost of tuition. As Old Man Potter told George Bailey in *It's a Wonderful Life*, "You're worth more dead than alive!"

"Just think about it, will you?" she asked.

"OK," I said, but I already had my answer.

It wasn't officially Father's Day. Steph had suggested moving it up several weeks, so it wouldn't conflict with the Price family reunion being held that same holiday weekend in June. I now suspected the real reason she'd changed the date was to make it possible for her to raise the baby issue when I was emotionally vulnerable. *Could he really reject being a father on Father's Day?*

Perhaps I was being paranoid, and I tried to let it go, but then Steph and the boys organized a Father's Day picnic in the backyard. This was a nice gesture, but unusual—perhaps another passive-aggressive effort to convince me to add another mouth to feed? If so, it backfired. Steph's request had made me newly sensitive to how our resources were already insufficient to support the family we had. House, income, even the picnic blanket—it was barely big enough to hold the four of us. This doesn't seem like a big deal, but you add one more person, even a small person, to an undersized picnic blanket, and suddenly everyone's legs are dangling over into the grass, inviting chigger bites and ticks. This is why I never liked being invited to picnics, especially if someone else volunteered to bring the blankets—there were never enough and/or they were always hopelessly undersized. *A beach towel is not a picnic blanket!* And then there was the standard picnic food, which inevitably involved some combination of mayonnaise, eggs, and meat—items that easily went south in the hot midwestern sun. More than once, I'd witnessed family and friends spend their post-picnic hours kneeling over a toilet bowl, simultaneously scratching the chigger bites on their ankles.

But like I said, the Father's Day picnic was a nice gesture.

Actually, it was a little early in the season to worry about chiggers, and I had to confess the backyard was at a very pretty stage. At some point in the summer, the greens of the lawn and trees would all sort of blend together, but now there appeared an infinite variety, from the black green of the spruce needles to the jade of the young oak leaves to the deep emerald of the grass. The few remaining periwinkles stood out like blue pinwheels in the margins, while Creeping Charlie, considered a weed by most, dotted the lawn with tiny lavender buttons. In the prairies of the Loess Hills, I wondered if the blue-eyed grass and the yucca were in bloom and, maybe in the secret places, the fringed orchids.

The sweet scent of the lilies of the valley filled the air, and I was tempted to wander over to admire them up close. Then I remembered Spencer had recently found a dead robin in that corner of the yard, and it might not be good to remind him. He was crying when he showed it to us. It looked undamaged, perhaps dying from a collision with the dining room window. Steph and I also considered the possibility of West Nile virus, which is carried by mosquitos—dead birds can be a warning sign. The fear of West Nile had inspired some parents we knew to douse their children with massive fogs of bug spray before letting them go outside, if they let them outside at all.

Steph had often worried about what the author Richard Louv had termed "nature deficit disorder" in American children, resulting from their parents' inability to let go of fear—of injury, of disease, of human predators—and allow them to freely explore the outdoors. Standing above the dead bird in our own yard, however, we'd instantly started whispering about how to handle potentially infected bodies and whether we should dress the kids in long shirts and pants until, say, July. At that point, the risk of heat stroke would outweigh any danger from mosquitoes.

Spencer was concerned about something else altogether.

"Is that how Gramma K is going to look when she dies?" he asked. His tone was almost imploring, and I considered how peaceful the bird looked, as if it were sleeping. He wanted her death to look that way, and I guess so did I.

"Yes," I replied, "that's how she'll look."

That's when an ant decided to crawl over the bird's eyeball.

"Git it off her!" he demanded. "Git it off!"

I reached down and brushed it away, West Nile be damned.

The robin was just the latest example of Spencer's increasing obsession with death since finding out about Grandma. He hadn't asked us directly about it, but almost the moment he walked in the door after his visit to Fort Dodge, he began working on a series of new picture books starring his alter ego, Tony Johnson. Tony's adventures suddenly shifted from fun with animals and balloon parties to necromancy and the quest for immortality. The new titles he dictated to us included:

Tony Johnson Makes Dead People Alive, but NOT Zombies!

Tony Johnson Goes to Heaven and Brings Back Grandma K and Her Doggy and Walmart Broasted Chicken!

Tony Johnson and Baby Live Forever!

Spencer's obsession was even more evident outdoors, where the No-Kill Law was in a period of increased enforcement. He and Baby, newly immortal, took regular shifts patrolling the yard, looking for potential infractions by those playing there as well as opportunities to dish out an ounce of prevention. He took all the bowls he could find in the kitchen, including china bowls from our wedding, and placed them over ant mounds in the driveway as protection. He gathered the sharpest sticks he could find and stuck them around the entrance to the woodchuck den to prevent "foxes and Neighbor Henry from crawling in there." He dragged out the old folding gate we'd used to block off the stairs when he was a baby and placed it in front of the honeyvine milkweed, where we found monarch caterpillars every year.

Spencer's efforts beyond the borders of our yard also increased. In the past, if we drove by dead animals in the street, there would be sad expressions, but we could keep moving. Now when Spencer spotted them, he would start pleading for us to stop and check the possum or raccoon or bird, because it might not be "all the way dead." There wasn't much choice—if we didn't stop, Spencer would unbuckle his seatbelt and try to open the door. Most of the time it was too late for heroics and some, like the giant, hissing snapping turtle, didn't seem to want our help. The previous week, however, Steph and the boys discovered a barely alive baby black squirrel in the middle of the road. Black squirrels are actually a protected species in Council Bluffs, a localized genetic mutation that has become the town mascot. It is illegal to harm or harass them within city limits. Legal responsibility for injured black squirrels halfway to roadkill was a little fuzzy, but not for Spencer: "Franklin" (named for the street where he was found) was immediately placed in the Spider-Man beach towel and taken to our house. Steph called several local wildlife rehabilitators, then traveled with Spencer all the way to a volunteer's home in West Omaha. Spencer regularly asked us to call and check on the little guy's status, which thankfully was improving.

But Spencer wasn't satisfied with just saving local wildlife. His master plan, apparently, was to expand the No-Kill Law to encompass the entire globe and all its creatures, including people. Recently, while I was watching the news about some distant natural disaster or human-made tragedy, Spencer snuck into the room, snagged the clicker, and turned off the television.

"There," he said. "Now all those people don't have to die."

How does a parent respond to this? We'd done our best to calm his fears, and had encouraged him to talk about his feelings, but he wasn't interested in talking. He was interested in *doing*.

Spencer's response to the robin was just the latest example, but it included a new and unexpected development. After Steph gave the bird the West Nile gloves-and-sandwich-baggie treatment, we gently laid the body in a small box and dug a hole among the day-lilies. The funeral ritual, at which we were now experts, included slowly lowering the coffin into the hole and offering a few words of respect. Individual dedications to the robin included such things as "she was a good flapper" and "she always tweeted a happy song in the morning" and "she will have a warm, twiggy nest in heaven."

After each testimonial, the person placed a flower in the grave, but when it came time for Spencer to say something, he was silent.

"You should'na did that," he finally said, staring into the hole.

His face was red with anger, and at first we thought he was mad about the fact of death, the fact that all of us, including robins and Grammas, have to die. But when Spencer threw his flower on the ground and stomped off, we realized he was mad at the bird. It was as if she had violated the No-Kill Law by dying in our back-yard, so close to his home and his heart.

As if she'd had a choice.

Back at the picnic, we'd finished eating—not a drop of mayon-naise anywhere—and I thought we'd managed to escape any re-minders of injury and death. Then Ben began reminiscing about his last birthday party in the backyard, when we'd inadvertently placed the Slip 'N Slide over some jagged walnut shells and sev-eral children, including Spencer, received bloody gashes. He then handed me his Father's Day present, which I guessed from the size was an action figure, a traditional gift from the boys on this holiday. They'd give me an action figure, and then play with it the rest of the day. I didn't mind. I had quite a collection of them as a kid, including a suitcase full of those eight-inch superheroes with the cloth tights and plastic gloves and boots that always got lost.

As I pulled back the wrapping paper, I expected to see yet another superhero. Instead, I found myself confronting the Headless Horseman from the Johnny Depp movie *Sleepy Hollow,* complete with bloody neck stump and two decapitated heads dangling from his clenched fist.

Spencer started whimpering.

"It's OK, Spence," I said, laughing nervously. "It's just fake, *hee-hee-hee.* It's just a doll."

His whimpering got louder, and then I noticed Baby sitting in his lap and remembered that, for Spencer, dolls can become real.

"I picked that out for you at the comic book store, Dad," Ben interjected. "Mom told me not to, but I told her you and me like monsters."

Actually that was true—yet another genetic flaw from my side. Grandpa Roy had been a big horror fan and kept a red-covered book in his basement full of photos from thriller movies: zombies eating human flesh, vampires sucking the necks of scantily clad women, and a guy with an axe planted in the middle of his head, to describe just a few. Whenever my younger cousin David visited Fort Dodge, Grandpa would let us go down to his basement, get out the red book and the markers, and start copying the bloody scenes. They became part of our own illustrated horror stories in which we were the heroes, conquering one deadly evil after another. Grandpa actually seemed pleased by our interest, perhaps because the "thriller gene" had skipped a generation—our fathers hated those movies—and reemerged in David and me.

And now Ben.

"Thanks, buddy," I said, quietly putting it behind my back. "We'll have a lot of, uh, fun with that."

The next gift was from Steph. Guessing from the shape of the package, it looked to be a CD, and I had my hopes about it. The week before, I'd been complaining I didn't have enough time to keep up with the contemporary music scene—the last CD I'd purchased was by R.E.M. in the midnineties. She asked if I'd heard anything good on the radio, and I remembered liking a song by a group called the Black Rebel Motorcycle Club. Their style reminded me of a combination of Led Zeppelin and the garage bands I'd followed in my twenties. And their name seemed tailor-made for a guy experiencing a midlife crisis.

I ripped off the wrapping paper and found a CD by . . . the Black Eyed Peas. I tried to look pleased and turned it over to peruse the song list. *My Humps?* Was that another reference to pregnancy?

"That's the group you were talking about, right?" Steph asked.

"Well . . ." but before I could finish, she began to tear up again.

"Here's my gift, Daddy," Spencer said, still sniffling.

It was a small book, *Father to Son: Life Lessons on Raising a Boy,* by Harry H. Harrison, Jr. It was full of short snippets of wisdom the author felt fathers should be teaching their sons. This was the kind of novelty book I usually hated, in which the writers offered cutesy advice for others, but never themselves.

"Thanks!"

"Momma said you'd like it," Spencer said. I tried to thank her, too, but she was too busy not looking at me.

I opened the book to a random page and read it out loud: "'Teach him that self-pity is a waste of time.'"

Nice sentiment, I thought, but sometimes I found self-pity to be a very satisfying way to spend the day. This was another trait I'd apparently passed on to Ben.

"Hey, this isn't fair," he said, crossing his arms.

"What are you talking about?" I asked.

"It's not fair that grown-ups have THREE present days and kids only have TWO. WE only have Christmas and birthdays and I think there should be a Happy KIDS Day."

I was about to laugh, derisively, but then I felt a tickle on my neck, which is another bad thing on a picnic. I quickly brushed it onto the grass, and was relieved to see it was only a daddy long-legs. As a kid, I'd heard that daddy longlegs are the most venomous spiders in the world but have no fangs to inject the poison. I found out later they're neither spiders nor venomous. Perhaps because of this, they get no respect and have become the playthings of children on picnics. Grown-ups like me simply brush them away.

"Daddy killed the spider!" Spencer wailed.

"What? It's not a spider, Spencer, and I didn't kill it."

He kept on crying.

"Spencer, this is ridiculous—I didn't hurt the daddy longlegs. See, it's crawling right over there and. . . ." That's when I noticed it was now crawling with a decided limp, barely making its way through the forest of grass, and so did everyone else. Spencer squeezed the sides of his skull in despair. Steph glared at me.

"The more I think about it, Ben," she said, "the more I think a Kids Day is a great idea. And the first tradition will be for you and your father to go exchange his apparently awful CD for something you and Spencer would like."

"Yay!"

On the way to the store, I considered how every child in America had tried out the "Kids Day" argument. Now, apparently, we were going to be the first parents to actually give in. Ben couldn't believe his good luck and was thinking out loud about how best to celebrate this new holiday. Since there's only one father getting gifts on Father's Day, he reasoned there should be only one kid getting presents on a particular Kids Day. The first holiday, today, would be called "International Ben Day," and the second, date yet to be determined, would be called "International Spencer Day."

"Why International?" I asked.

"Because people in China will want to have it too. Maybe parades and everything!"

This was indeed a milestone for children everywhere.

When we entered the doors of the electronics store, Ben shot off to the DVD section. By the time I caught up, he'd decided on a collection of classic Warner Bros. cartoons, which he claimed Spencer would also like. I had to admit I wouldn't mind seeing some of those old childhood favorites. At the register, I handed over the Black Eyed Peas CD for the exchange but still owed a little money. I reached into my pocket and discovered I'd left my wallet at home. Then I recalled that Grandma K had given Ben a five-dollar bill when he was in Fort Dodge, and that he'd been carrying it everywhere with him, rolled up with a yellow rubber band around it.

"Hey Ben, could you loan me your five-dollar bill so I can get the DVD?"

"No."

"Excuse me?"

"Gramma K gave it to me."

"I know, but I'll pay you right back when we get home."

He looked at me like I wasn't getting the point.

"Gramma K gave it to me, and I won't let you have it."

His voice was raised, and the other people in line stopped talking and began to stare.

"You're not *giving* it to me, Ben, you're just *loaning* it to me. I'll pay you back when we get home."

"You can't have my money from Gramma K!" he yelled, and I could feel the stares of the other customers burning into my neck. They must have thought I was trying to steal money from my own child.

"That's ridiculous!" Now my voice was raised.

"Sir," the sales clerk interrupted. "Perhaps I can hold it for you until you come back."

"Fine!" I slammed the DVD onto the counter and marched Ben back to the car. No words were exchanged on the drive home. I walked inside, past Spencer and Steph, who were once again not looking at me, retrieved my wallet, got back in the car, and returned to the store, again in complete silence. Ben and I stood in line for a long time—some guy was asking the sales clerk a laundry list of questions about his new computer—and by the time we arrived at the counter, I was furious. The overly polite look from the clerk, who'd witnessed my earlier performance, didn't help. I finally completed the exchange and handed the DVD to Ben:

"Happy Goddamned International Ben Day!"

"Thanks," he replied in a perfectly pleasant voice. "Can we watch this when we get home? I love Bugs Bunny."

Later, while stretched out in the bedroom, the voice of Foghorn Leghorn leaking up from the living room—"That dog, I say that dog's strictly GI: Gibberin' Idiot, that is"—I considered what clearly wasn't one of my best moments as a father. Why had I reacted in such a stupid way? The book Spencer had given me, *Father to Son*, was on the bed stand, and perhaps hoping to further torture myself, I picked it up. I wasn't disappointed. Each section offered plenty of wisdom I'd failed to pass on to my sons. I had not, for instance, taught them how to use carpentry tools, how to floss, how to read the financial page in the newspaper, how to meditate, or how to spit. On the other hand, I had been pretty good at making them laugh, displaying their artwork in my office, giving hugs before bedtime, telling them often that I love them, and teaching them not to litter. It was also likely that, before the day was through, I would demonstrate "how to apologize."

What I was most struck by, however, was all the wisdom listed in the book that my sons were trying to teach me. They had taken their father "for walks and introduced him to bugs," and invited him "to go barefoot," "to play outdoors a lot," and to "get wet and dirty." Through their presence in my life, and our adventures in the No-Kill Zone, they had strengthened my conviction "not to hurt others," and encouraged me to see "every life as precious" and "each day as holy." Even when I failed to do so.

It seemed, as well, that fatherhood had been teaching me that I am, in the words of Tibetan Buddhist master Chögyam Trungpa, "living in a rich world, one that never runs out of messages." The problem was that I'd mostly been ignoring them. There were long stretches when no matter what I *did* as a father, good or bad, what I *felt* was less like a father and more like a daddy longlegs, a creature always running away from a challenge, yet always finding himself in situations that threatened to overwhelm. A creature who, despite all the stories and myths about his power, was powerless to control anything.

Lying there in bed, however, I decided that for once I wouldn't run away. I would stay still and be there for whatever thoughts and feelings floated my way.

The first "message" to arrive was in the form of that five-dollar bill. It was clear Ben would never spend it—that's how much it meant to him—but what did it mean to me, other than shame over mistreating my five-year-old? Of course, shame was nothing unusual in my relationship with money. I'd often felt ashamed I didn't make more of it, ashamed I hadn't been the kind of provider my family deserved, and then ashamed for feeling that way. Steph had never made me feel that way. It was a seemingly immutable aspect of my nature.

The more I thought about it, though, the more Ben's five-dollar bill began to offer up a different notion of value. I began to imagine it as an almost living thing, with its own remarkable story. After escaping the walls of the U.S. Treasury, it had traveled for years, perhaps across the globe, being spent on one thing or another, one appetite or another, until finally landing in the hands of an elderly Iowa woman. Then, somewhere in the space between her hand and her great-grandson's, it had taken on a new and completely unexpected value. Now, because of that value, it would no longer be spent on material objects or appetites, because it was already being spent, every day, on the love that exists between two people.

But was there a limit to even that kind of currency? How much of it did I actually have to spend? Here I landed back on the question of bringing yet another life into the world. There was a time, just before we conceived Ben, when I wanted nothing more than to have a child. I felt that again with Spencer. What had changed, beyond the practical circumstances of our lives? Was it really about limited resources, financial, physical, or otherwise? Was it even about having another child?

What value was being held before me, to hoard or to spend?

I broke off the barrage of questions and picked up the little book Spencer had given me. I opened to another page:

"The only way to confront fear is to walk through it."

Or *limp* through it, I thought. Like the daddy longlegs, on whatever legs we have left, in the only direction that may be available to us: Out of one moment and into the next.

10

No-Kill Alert: Niña, the Chihuahua

"I WANT YOU to promise me something, John."

Grandma was sitting on her couch at Friendship Haven, petting Niña. The tiny dog was snuggled into her lap, having just exhausted itself barking and nipping at my ankles. Her black, bug eyes were fixed on me suspiciously—I almost felt compelled to explain to her my unexpected visit, which was fairly spur-of-the-moment. My mother had recently informed me that Grandma had stopped eating. She just wasn't hungry anymore, she said. I worried the end might be near, so I dropped everything and drove to Fort Dodge. When I showed up, I was surprised to see that although thinner, Grandma seemed to have actually gained vitality. She was almost regal, dressed in a white pantsuit with a tassled white shawl and Mexican turquoise-and-silver jewelry dangling everywhere.

There was command in her voice.

"Anything, Grandma."

"I want you to promise to take care of Niña after I'm gone, and adopt her into your family."

"Uh, I'm not sure about that," I said, but what I really meant to say was, *You've got to be fucking kidding me!* First, Steph wants another baby, now this? Does my grandmother have any clue how we're living? How could I explain to her we have no room in our lives for a dog, even one that can live comfortably inside a glove compartment?

"Well, I want your answer soon," Grandma continued, "otherwise I'm going to have her euthanized and buried with me."

"Like the Egyptian queens?"

"What was that?"

"Nothing."

"Well, all I know is. . . ." Her voice started breaking.

Oh God, I thought, she's crying—I've made my dying grandmother cry. I'm making everyone cry these days.

"I'm not saying I won't, Grandma." *What was I doing?* "I'm just saying I'm not sure, because . . . because. . . ." She and Niña glared at me. I thought I heard a tiny growl.

"Because . . . you've given so much love to each other, I just want to make sure she's with someone who can give her the special kind of love she needs."

Grandma's face relaxed a little. "That's true—*isn't it, sweet-ums?*" She took the dog's mug in her palms and kissed its tiny black lips. "No one loves you like I do, do they? And no one loves me like you do."

This statement clearly pleased the dog, which wagged its little fan tail and furiously licked my grandmother's mouth, but it rubbed me the wrong way. What did she mean no one loved her like that dog? I'd just dropped everything to drive nearly two hundred miles to see her, leaving behind two little boys who were hanging on to every scrap of what remained of her, seemingly fighting against her death with every insect they saved, every ant-covered bird they mourned. And just across town, my mother was working her way through yet another stack of Grandma's insurance forms and financial statements and medical bills while facing the loss of her one remaining parent.

I was tempted to offer Grandma a little reality check about just what kind of love she enjoyed. Then I reconsidered the scene before me: on a plush floral couch, my ninety-two-year-old grandmother was being French-kissed by a Chihuahua.

This wasn't about reality.

"So," I said, "tell me more about Niña. Did you name her after your mother, Nina?"

She stiffened. "Certainly not. I would never name a dog after my mother. Niña means 'little girl' in Spanish. I love her almost as much, though—*don't I, Cutie*? Have I ever told you about my mother? She was a wonderful woman, John, smart and beautiful. Her one fault was that she made bad choices in men. My father was Bad Choice Number One."

She then launched with surprising force into the story of life after her childhood in Chicago, after her father, Clifford Hobson, had abandoned them. I'd heard pieces of this story before, but it was hard for me to keep all the places and people and grievances straight. My grandmother, with Niña's wet encouragement, appeared eager to finally set the record straight.

Grandma said she was around five when she and her mother and little sister, Virginia, moved back to her grandparents' house in Lehigh, Iowa, just southeast of Fort Dodge. J. W. and Josephine Porter, her grandparents, had met in the small western Iowa town of Defiance, not too far from where I was living now. Josie was the daughter of a local farmer who had moved the family, in covered wagon, from Kentucky to Illinois and then to the prairies of western Iowa. On one of those trips, when Josie was very young, she got a piece of "barley shaft" in her eye, which festered and left her permanently cross-eyed. With little hope of marriage, she became the family servant, washing their clothes and taking care of her sisters' babies. She was denied schooling and piano lessons, except what she could pick up from the books and sheet music her siblings brought home.

Josie was serving refreshments at a barn dance when she met James William Porter—J. W. for short—who was a local farmhand, telegrapher, and fiddle player. He was an orphan, my grandmother told me, who revealed very little of his past other than he'd spent part of his boyhood on an "eastern wharf." Grandma suspected he may have arrived here on one of the orphan trains, which carried poor kids from Eastern cities out West to work on farms, but she didn't know for sure.

The bottom line was neither J. W. nor Josie had much of a past worth remembering. Only a future, which they decided to risk together.

They moved to Lehigh, a gypsum and coal mining community along the Des Moines River, where J. W. started a very successful butcher shop and slaughterhouse. He purchased large tracts of farmland in Iowa and Minnesota, built the local Masonic Temple, and, for good measure, bought the silent picture theater where Josie could finally play piano to her heart's content. He also bought her fine dresses from Paris and paraded her around town in a fancy carriage, which didn't fail to earn the ire of some locals.

"One time, when she was walking downtown, some miners spit on her dress for acting so high and mighty," Grandma told me.

She remembered the Porter home as a beautiful Victorian "house on a hill," where she and Virginia ate off china dishes with silver and walked in silk stockings across wood floors that shined like mirrors. Grandma Josie, who'd been denied an education as a child, had her own library, where a young Kathryn lost herself in many works of classic literature. Josie's complete set of Dickens remained on the shelves in my parents' home, from which I'd read several volumes.

Unfortunately, it didn't last. According to Grandma, the Porters' downfall was due in part to overindulging their three children: Paul, Nina, and Tommy. As a teenager, Nina ran off with a baseball star, then returned to Lehigh with no husband and two daughters, all of whom lived with her parents. Soon after, Paul, the eldest, died from pneumonia, leaving a widow and two daughters. J. W. had loaned Paul the money to purchase his farm—against Josie's wishes—and it now needed tending. So he sold the house on the hill and moved everyone to Paul's old farmhouse, where the floors didn't shine so bright. They eventually sold that farm at a loss and moved to another one. Meanwhile, their youngest son, Tommy, was racking up huge debts while attending Drake University in Des Moines.

The family needed more money, so Nina quit her job as a local teacher and took a position at a department store in Fort Dodge. She visited her daughters on the weekends.

"After my mother left every Sunday to go back to Fort Dodge, I would go upstairs to a closet, shut the door, and cry. I missed her so much. Virginia was too young to really know what was going on, and she loved it on the farm. My grandparents adored her—they'd practically raised her from birth. I suppose I *was* jealous. I'd come home from school and see her following Grandpa around the barn and he'd tell me cute stories about the stuff they'd done together. I'd just go back up to the closet and cry for my mother."

In Fort Dodge, Nina was being courted by Frank D., an Oldsmobile dealer almost twenty years her senior. She'd put him off for several years—he had a reputation as a gambler—but finally relented when he promised to bring the family together and support them in style. Turned out "style" was a small apartment in the Warden Plaza, where the beds were separated by nothing but a sheet.

"You think you live in cramped conditions," she said. "I was eleven or so when Virginia and I moved there from Lehigh, and I heard things that, well, let's just say I'd rather forget."

The family eventually moved into a larger apartment, and the future was looking bright. In high school, Grandma always had nice clothes and a new car to show off from her stepfather's dealership. But then Frank's gambling debts came due, and he begged his father-in-law for a loan. J. W. gave it to him but never saw the money again. After Nina finally divorced him, Frank shot himself—or was "executed"—in the basement of the Warden. No one knew for sure, which led to a lot of talk that hurt the family, because not knowing the reasons didn't stop people from handing out blame. J. W. must have foreseen what was coming. In partial payment of his debt, he had required Frank to pay Virginia's nursing school tuition at the State University of Iowa.

"Why didn't you get the college education?" I asked. "You were the oldest."

This part of the story always infuriated me. My grandmother had been a talented student, and according to her high school yearbook, had loved literature, Latin, writing poetry, and reporting for the school newspaper. She loved learning—still loved it. Ever since I could remember, she'd been mailing me newspaper and magazine clippings on subjects she thought I might find interesting, from literature to religion to science to politics. She then called, repeatedly, to ask my opinion about the articles or to hound me into reading them. I sometimes referred to it as "intellectual harassment."

And yet, when pressed to defend or explain her own ideas, my grandmother would often reply, "Oh, I don't know anything." Some might have interpreted this self-deprecation as a sign of humility, or even stubbornness, but for me it was just another answer to Langston Hughes's famous question: "What happens to a dream deferred?"

"Your mother and grandparents should have stood up for you," I continued. "Especially your grandmother Josie, who knew what it was like to be passed over. You should have had the chance."

"Oh, I don't know," she replied. "I do remember crying in the doorway when Virginia left for college—I wanted to go so badly. But that's just the way it was."

So she stayed home and fell in love with a Fort Dodge boy, Harold "Andy" Anderson, the son of Swedish immigrants. My future grandfather. During the Depression, he had a decent job reading meters for the Iowa–Illinois Gas and Electric and a yellow Ford coupe, but he'd also earned a reputation for partying.

"He was such a good dancer," she said, "and brought such fun into my life, I just fell for him."

They were married in 1936, and moved into the Biltwell Apartments just across from the Methodist church. The proximity did nothing to discourage my grandfather's rowdy social life. Grandma was working ten to twelve hours at the candy counter in Kresge's Five and Dime, and one evening she came home to find his friends packed into the living room, "raising hell"—drinking liquor, spilling it on her carpet and furniture, and getting sick in their bathroom. When the parties became a regular event, she told Andy it was them or her.

"It was humiliating, John. The mornings after those parties, on his way to work, Andy would ask the landlady, 'Well, who complained this time?' She liked us, otherwise we would have been out in the street. We moved to a rental house, away from his friends, but your grandfather never entirely gave up the drinking. That was the case for a lot of men back then who had that disease—they didn't have any help."

In 1940, their only child, Sondra, my mother, was born, and they eventually moved to the upper floor of a house on the corner of North 9th Street and Dakota, owned by Virginia and her husband, Wallace. Virginia had a daughter, Ginny Kay, about the same age as Sondra. Their youngest child, Billy, suffered from Hirschsprung's disease. Wallace worked in Chicago for long stretches, and Virginia was a full-time nurse in Fort Dodge, so my grandmother often took care of Billy, who was just a toddler. She massaged his distended belly and comforted him at night when he screamed from the pain, singing to him and holding his face up to the moon. She told him it was the face of God. He was only two when he died.

"I fell to pieces," she said. "And you know what Wallace told me after the funeral? He said, 'I hope you don't expect me to repay you for taking care of Billy.' I couldn't believe it. I never wanted anything from him—I loved that little boy as if he were my own."

Wallace, Virginia, and Ginny Kay soon moved to Chicago. Once again, my grandmother remained in Fort Dodge, where, one by one, she took care of everyone else in the family. First, her grandfather J. W. Porter, who suffered from congestive heart disease. By that time, he and Josie had moved to a little house in nearby Otho. Thanks to the Depression—as well as the various debts associated with their children and their spouses—they'd lost the properties in Lehigh and the farmland and were down to almost nothing in the bank. All that was left was a garden and a chicken coop, and Kathryn and Andy came out every weekend to help tend them.

When the end finally came, J. W. called my grandmother to his bedside, took her hand, and made her promise to take care of her grandma Josie.

"I promised," she said, "and then he closed his eyes and died. He must have known something, because not long after that, Grandmother began to lose her mind."

Nina, in order to help care for her mother, temporarily moved back to Iowa from Seattle, where she'd relocated with Mistake Number Three, Russell M. They moved Josie into the downstairs of the house on North 9th Street, in the apartment below my grandparents and my mother. Nina stayed there for well over a year. My mother was just a child, but she recalls her grandma Nina always wanting to be cuddled at bedtime, as if she were the child. One night when they were in bed together, Josie burst into the room with a butcher knife and tried to kill Nina. Kathryn rushed downstairs, pulled her screeching grandmother off her mother and daughter, and held her on the ground until help arrived. Mom was eight when she witnessed this, and would forever after refuse to watch horror films.

Josie was put in a straitjacket and taken to the hospital, and Nina reluctantly returned to Seattle. During the next couple of years, Kathryn regularly visited her grandmother in the county home.

"I felt so bad she was out there. All she had was a bed in a large commons area, full of people who screamed and cried all the time.

I would take Sondra to visit her every Sunday. We'd bring her fruit and ice cream and play her favorite songs on the piano, especially 'The Little Brown Jug.' Sondra and I would sing, which she loved. I still felt I'd broken my promise to Grandpa, and hadn't taken care of her the way he would've wanted. I feel that way today."

After Josie passed away, Nina started suffering from mysterious ailments. It got so bad Kathryn decided to go to Seattle to help her mother for a few weeks in the summer, and brought along Sondra, who'd just turned ten. While out there, she took Nina to see a doctor. He called my grandmother into his office, alone, where he revealed that Nina had inoperable cancer. Six months to live, tops. He told her not to reveal this to Nina, as it would only make things worse.

For the next few weeks, Kathryn nursed her mother, lying about the prognosis and dealing with Russell, who kept badgering her to sign over any inheritance to him so he could pay the medical bills. She finally relented.

"Virginia was mad at me, but I was distraught, John. I just wanted Russell and everyone to leave me alone so I could be with my mother. That's all I ever wanted."

At the end of the summer, Andy told her she had to come back to Iowa. He needed her, and Sondra would be starting school soon. At the Seattle train station, a railroad official broke the rules and wheeled Nina up near the tracks so she could wave good-bye. It was the last time Kathryn would see her mother alive, and she knew it. Nina died a few months later, at age fifty-four.

"I cried on that train all the way back to Iowa," she said. "Your poor mother—she was just a little girl and didn't know what to do. She tried to comfort me, bless her heart, which is more than anyone else did. When we got off at the Fort Dodge station, I was still crying, and your grandfather told me I was a damn fool for acting that way. I never forgave him for that, never. . . ."

Grandma put her face in her hands and sobbed. Niña looked at her, then at me, then back at her and began to shake.

"I'm sorry," she said to me, or to the dog. "It's still hard for me to think about it. I loved my mother so much. That was a very dark time for me—Grandma and Grandpa, Billy, my mother, then Virginia. Poor Virginia. . . ."

History seemed to repeat itself for Grandma's little sister. While living in Chicago, Wallace left Virginia for his secretary. She moved to Seattle with Ginny Kay, then Canada, where she got remarried. Following several surgeries, she became addicted to painkillers. My grandmother and others attempted to help her get off the medications, even driving her to the Mayo Clinic in Minnesota, but the pain was too much, and she eventually committed suicide. Virginia, like her mother, died in her early fifties.

"On top of all that," Grandma continued, "your grandfather retires, we move to Arizona, and he almost immediately suffers a stroke. I'd been after him for years to give up the drinking, to get healthy, but no one could ever tell him what to do. Now the doctors weren't sure he'd ever walk again. I was completely alone with all of this in Arizona, John. Completely alone. Finally, I just collapsed on the bathroom floor and screamed and screamed at God that I couldn't take it anymore. I said I was turning it all over to Him, whether He liked it or not. That's not easy to do—my mother refused to do it, even at the end. She was too angry, but I had a feeling God would answer my prayer."

From where I was sitting, it was hard to say how or when her prayer had been answered, if at all. She ended up caring for my grandfather for almost twenty years while they lived in Arizona, helping him with the painful physical therapy, taking him to countless appointments, carefully monitoring his medicines and diet, driving him on little excursions to restaurants and museums and parks, trying to keep him engaged with life. He eventually progressed enough to walk with a cane, but then he fell at the swimming pool, broke his hip, and was mostly confined to his recliner in front of the television. He soon began suffering from dementia.

Grandma finally admitted she'd reached the limits of what she could do for him, and in 1994 they moved back to Fort Dodge.

Grandpa was admitted to a local nursing home, sharing a room with his sister, Esther, while Grandma rented a place in the nearby Dodger Apartments, only a block away from my parents.

In Fort Dodge, my grandmother was, for the first time, free from taking care of anyone in her family. It nearly drove her crazy. She spent most of her days at the nursing home with Grandpa and Esther and then, in the evenings, obsessively calling my parents to ask questions about his care or to panic about medical bills or to criticize people for not visiting him more often—especially my mother, who was working full-time and raising my youngest sister, Allyson, who was still a teenager.

Things got even worse after Grandpa died in 1998, as she sunk into a deep depression. Then a friend of my mother's offered to give Grandma one of their newborn Chihuahua puppies, and everything changed. Perhaps this was the answered prayer she was referring to: in the hour of need, she'd been delivered yet another creature to whom she could give herself entirely. She showered Niña with devotion, knitting her colorful snuggies, hand-feeding her Walmart broasted chicken, and even providing her with a private puppy pad behind the couch, so she, too, didn't have to suffer the indignity of wetting herself in public. Niña returned that devotion, waiting for my grandmother in bed every night, curling up on the pillow next to her head and remaining there until morning. That dog never voluntarily left my grandmother's side. Never.

My mother could have hardly known that in giving a Chihuahua to Grandma, she was bringing a rival sibling into the family. Grandma often referred to Niña as "Sondra's baby sister." She rarely brought her over to my parents' house, however, claiming Niña hated my father. She hated almost everyone, but that didn't stop Grandma from publicly blaming my father, as if this were evidence that, despite being active in church and dedicating much of his life to helping the poor, there was still some major flaw at the core of his character. Grandma regularly turned down invitations to visit my sisters and me and her great-grandchildren, because it would involve taking Niña to the kennel like an ordinary pet. She made an exception for Spencer's birth, visiting us in the hospital, but only because my father agreed to drive her back again the same evening—six hours, round-trip—so she could fall asleep with her "little girl."

In many ways, though, that dog was the answer to my mother's prayers, relieving some of the pressures and responsibilities, just as a real sibling might. While Mom took care of Grandma's endless insurance forms and medical appointments and shopping, Niña took care of her round-the-clock need for love and attention.

Niña was a troublemaker, however, and like others in Grandma's life, had earned a bit of a local reputation. When Grandma was living in the Dodger Apartments, Niña nipped a neighbor child, and the landlord forced her to contain the dog inside a chicken-wire enclosure whenever she went outdoors.

"Like a common criminal!" she protested.

Another time, when Grandma was taking her for a walk, Niña began barking at a free-roaming Labrador, apparently forgetting she was the size of a large gerbil. The Lab, usually a friendly breed, finally got fed up, bit the leash, and dragged both Niña and my grandmother a good five yards down the sidewalk. Both were treated at their respective hospitals.

As my grandmother's health-care needs increased, Mom tried to find her an assisted living facility, but most turned her down when they discovered the old woman and the dog were a package deal. By the time Friendship Haven announced they would be building a brand new wing, a doctor had designated Niña a "therapeutic necessity" for her depression (which she certainly was). Mom acquired an apartment for Grandma at the far end of the hall, but that didn't prevent her "therapeutic necessity" from nipping some of the other residents who made the mistake of trying to pet her.

"It's their own fault," Grandma told us, after being gently reprimanded by management. "They come at her with their hands, like this. . . ." She made a claw and jammed it in our faces. "Everybody knows the proper way to approach a dog is with palm open, on the ground, so they have a chance to sniff you."

I wanted to reply that three-quarters of the residents at Friendship Haven were incapable of bending over to tie their shoes, let alone rest the back of their hand on the floor and wait for a rat dog to sniff it and grant its approval. Weren't there enough indignities to growing old in this society?

Still, in the end, we were all grateful to Niña for what she'd done for Grandma, and would never allow her to be prematurely euthanized. The question was who would be foolish enough to take her in once Grandma was gone? Who was going to risk the barking and flesh wounds and lawsuits? Who was going to suffer soaked puppy pads behind their couch, midnight chicken runs to Walmart, and daily walks that might end with getting dragged down the sidewalk by a large dog?

"Well, she can't go to your parents," my grandmother repeated from her throne on the couch. "Your father absolutely *hates* Niña—I just can't understand it. What's wrong with the world?"

In that moment, it became clear to me that what my grandmother couldn't understand had little to do with my father or me or anyone else. What she couldn't understand was the collective human failure to love, to know what love demands—to serve, to sacrifice, to give everything to someone else and be entirely, irrevocably changed, transformed, consumed. As she had been with her grandparents, her mother, her nephew, her sister, her husband. She was right, that kind love was hard to find in the world today, perhaps since the high point of her generation—"The Greatest," as some have called it. Perhaps even longer, like since Christ died on the cross.

"Now I'm going to die and the one thing I've asked is for someone to take care of Niña, and no one will do it."

"I'm not saying I won't, Grandma."

And I almost believed I would do it, or at least try. I could have challenged her with that, with all the ways people were trying, but what was there to say?

She held the dog's face up to her own and repeated the truth of it: "No one loves me like you do, do they, *sweetums*? Do they?"

11

Motherfisher

AT MY FRIEND Andy's wedding, the maid of honor's toast included a graphic description of a pap smear.

"The first time I met our lovely bride her legs were in the stirrups," she said. "I was a physician's assistant and the doctor was moving his hand in and out between her thighs, commenting about how firm her cervix was. . . ."

As best man, I considered this might be a hard act to follow. When she finally sat down, I gathered my courage.

"The first time I met Andy," I said into the microphone, "we were four, it was summer, and he was tearing past my yard on a bike with a missing seat. Suddenly, he turned around and shouted out that he was going to Cal Woods Pharmacy to get himself a Charms sucker, and would I want one too. We've been best friends ever since."

I went on to say how remarkable it was that we now lived only a few miles from each other. Andy, I told the guests, had provided a friendship through the years that, like that of a brother, was reliable and unconditional. No matter how long we were apart, when we got back together, we simply picked up the conversation of our lives, and our mutual affection, as if no time had passed. As an added bonus, Andy fixed my car and lawnmower for free, as generous as he was on the first day we met.

I raised my glass to him and Julissa, wished them a lifetime of happiness, and sat down.

As the conversations and tinkling of silverware resumed, I considered all the ways my toast failed to communicate what our friendship meant to me, and how much I regretted neglecting it over the last year or so. But when I looked at Andy, his face reassured me that appreciating our history did not require words. At least for us. Our friendship just existed, a living, enduring thing that was not, we knew, born out of a love for candy but out of tragedy.

In 1974, a few months after my brother was stillborn, Andy's father, a crop duster, was killed when his plane crashed into a cornfield. We were in the third grade. We never really talked about these losses with each other—children weren't encouraged to talk about such things at the time—but I believe they nonetheless synchronized our ways of looking at the world, drawing us closer, distinguishing us from the other, untouched children. We no longer considered life a given, for one. It could, as we knew, change or disappear in a single stroke, the cause of which was beyond anyone's understanding. Our responses were different, however. Andy often appeared detached, unwilling to invest a great deal of emotion in anything or anyone. For that he was praised for being "laid-back" and "easygoing" or criticized for not being a "go-getter." I, in turn, engaged in a kind of hyperactive magical-realism, inventing imaginary companions, drawing out comic book adventures in which I had incredible powers over life and death. For that, I was praised for being "creative" or criticized for being "unrealistic" or "a dreamer." Andy ended up working with machines; I ended up working with stories.

While dancing with Steph during the wedding reception, I looked over at my friend, who in middle age had finally found the love he'd searched for. I'd found that love earlier in my life, but it had been just as unlikely. When we first met, Steph was eighteen and I was twenty-one. During my sister Carrie's college graduation in Missouri, I saw her across the dormitory cafeteria, made inquiries, and, quite out of character, sent a letter of introduction to her home in Idaho. She sent me a friendly reply, and for the next few months we exchanged more letters, building to a phone conversation, and then an actual meeting while she was visiting her grandparents in Iowa for Thanksgiving. She moved here the next summer, and three years later, we got married. We've been together ever since.

Told like this, the story seemed inevitable, irrevocable, and sometimes—too often, really—that's how I'd seen it. When it came to my marriage, I'd forgotten what the universe had revealed to me as a boy. But something had happened that week to remind me: Steph had discovered another lump in her breast.

This in itself wasn't enough to tip everything over—she'd had many lumps in the time I'd known her, having been diagnosed with fibrocystic tissue years ago. Since we'd gotten married, she'd had two excisional biopsies, both of them benign. She'd continued to be vigilant, however, especially after several other women in her family were diagnosed with breast cancer, including her sister, two aunts, and two first cousins diagnosed in their thirties. One of those cousins, Lynda, who'd videotaped our wedding, lost her life to it, leaving behind a husband and child.

This new lump seemed to confirm our worst fears. The doctor was so concerned by what she saw in the ultrasound that she immediately took a biopsy and scheduled an appointment, where she would share the results. She insisted we attend together because, as she said, "the news could be bad."

"Prepare yourselves."

As I held Steph during the slow dance, it seemed as if her body had at once become lighter and more substantial. If I could only hold her closer, tighter, maybe I would suffocate whatever was growing inside her. Or, at the very least, suffocate the thought of losing her.

"Jeez, John," she said. "This isn't junior high. The next thing you'll grab my butt and start licking my ear."

"I love you," I said.

She pulled back, smiled, and put her hand on my cheek.

You'd think a moment like this would be enough for a person, but the next day it was clear Steph intended to test its sincerity.

"I want to go fishing with the boys," she said. "And I want you to come with."

"Sure," I replied. "Absolutely."

This may not seem like a big deal unless you know, as she did, that I hate fishing. Steph grew up in Idaho, camping and casting with generations of her family, while my Iowa family "camped out" in air-conditioned motel rooms. When we ate fish, which was rarely, it came from the store in neat frozen cubes or tucked into breading and baked into something resembling a giant french fry. "Fish," as I had known them, did not swim in lakes and rivers but in a sea of tartar.

Many of my friends, however, including Andy, were enthusiastic fishermen and seemed to actually relish getting up in the cold dark with their various fathers to collect earthworms and spend a day casting into a lake. Or even more impressive, drilling a hole into the ice above that same lake, then sitting over that hole for several freezing hours waiting for something to happen. If I'd been older, I might have seen a correlation between ice fishing and writing. As it was, though, I assumed there must be something truly wonderful, magical even, about fishing if people were willing to go to such extremes.

Until I actually went fishing. I don't remember who I was with or how old I was, but I couldn't have been much more than seven or eight. What I do remember is the bone chill of the air before sunrise; the awkward, muddy launch of the boat; the sort of rancid-mildewy smell of the dark lake water—who knew what was lurking beneath the surface, waiting for me to fall in? There was, I admit, a slight thrill when casting the line, seeing how far it could go, but it was quickly followed by the soul-deadening tedium of sitting and watching, in complete silence, for a tremor in the bobber. During that long wait, I had time to once again contemplate the cold, the smell, the mud and water collecting in the bottom of the boat, creeping over my shoes, soaking my feet—did it seem to be rising?

Someone eventually got a bite, and I recall the anticipation of seeing what was on the end of the line, how big it was and all that, but of the creature itself I recall only a gaping mouth, opening and closing as it struggled to breathe. Then the sound, later, on the shore, of the hammer coming down on its head, and then the sound, like ripping fabric, of the knife slitting it from gills to tail, and then the awful smell and how it got on everyone's hands and stayed there for days, even mine, though I never touched the thing. It seemed to confirm (as if I didn't already know it) that death emitted a stench that covered everything in the vicinity, and which could never be washed out or escaped. Even if no one else noticed it but you.

Steph saw fishing a little differently. She fished with her father in the wild mountain streams of Idaho and with her grandfather in the placid ponds and rivers of Iowa. She loved fishing for all the reasons I hated it, especially the sense of shared solitude where no words were required or asked for, not even thoughts. Only presence. The one feeling we shared was an aversion to actually killing the fish, and under her father's guidance, she'd developed an almost elegant technique for catch-and-release that minimized injury without minimizing the sense of adventure. It began with the bait, which was usually fake lures or stink bait or corn kernels or, on occasion, wadded-up pieces of Wonder Bread. This is the reason Spencer had reacted so strongly to the worms being impaled on hooks during that fishing trip with our friends—though a veteran of the sport, he'd never witnessed such a wanton act of torture.

Also, the hook Steph used was small and smooth, which meant she lost a lot of fish, but those she did catch could be easily freed, with relatively little damage.

I had pointed out, on more than one occasion, that the hook still hurt the fish, that the struggle often injured it, and it was only going to get caught and eaten by someone else.

"The whole thing is hypocritical," I'd told her. "No matter what angle you look at it from."

"Sort of like life," she'd responded.

Ben and Spencer apparently agreed with her. Normally puritanical enforcers of their own version of ahimsa, the no-harm principle, they seemed willing to make an exception for fishing. During outdoor excursions in Iowa and Idaho (trips I'd often missed because of work or other "important" business I could no longer recall) Steph had taught them to appreciate the long stretches of waiting—not really waiting, she claimed, just "being"—during which it was possible to more fully appreciate the beauty of the world around them: the autumn leaf floating on the water, the morning music of birds, the splash of a jumping bass, the elegance of a heron's neck, the flare of a kingfisher in flight, the stark, brown-and-black decay of a branch extending into the water.

During those moments, their mother had not succeeded in teaching them to be hypocrites. She had taught them to look at the world with bigger eyes. Fish eyes.

The morning of the fishing trip, when Steph told the boys that their father would be coming along, they looked confused and a little anxious.

"Does he know the rules?" Ben asked.

"Don't worry," she replied. "We'll explain them to him."

On the way to their favorite fishing hole, Steph requested we take a detour along the Missouri River. I wasn't enthusiastic, given its current condition. In the days of Lewis and Clark, the Missouri had been a wide and slow-roaming river, its caramel waters swirling, eddying, in almost luxurious recline. Those waters had been home to an almost unbelievable diversity of life. In 1960 the flood-prone river was channeled by the Corps of Engineers, and that's when it began digging down into its body, scouring away what remained of its native identity, its memory, becoming too straight and fast for birds and people and other wildlife to spend much of their leisure there. It was now an ideal place for barge traffic, casinos, and suicides.

On the other side of the road from the river, through the early morning mist, we could just make out the dragon's spine of the Loess Hills, rising two hundred feet above the floodplain. The view of the hills from this road had always been inspiring for me, largely because the demands of driving only allowed for a quick glance, a peripheral awareness in which their mighty presence could exert a strong influence on the spirit, as it had with earlier explorers. In 1832, the artist George Catlin visited these hills and wrote: "Soul melting scenery that was about me! A place where the mind could think volumes; but the tongue must be silent that would speak, and hand palsied that would write. A place where a Divine would confess he never had fancied Paradise."

Catlin thought these "thousand thousand velvet-covered hills . . . tossing and leaping down with steep or graceful declivities to the river's edge, as if to grace its pictured shores . . ." ought to be part of the first American national park. Nearly forty years later, the mountains and forests of Yellowstone would earn that distinction.

The prairie still hung on in small remnants, gripping the western hillsides and nature-made terraces called "cat steps." Sometimes, when driving this road, I'd turn my head at the right moment and see that prairie, its distinguishing diversity of color and flutter of butterfly wings; or the magnificent hilltop oaks, remnants of the original savannah, stretching out their branches to better catch the sun. Another moment, however, and I'd see the suffocating presence of shrubs and red cedars and other invasives; or the enormous houses perched precariously on the crest of highly erodable, loess soil; or the crater of a landfill pit, the hillsides sliced in half, utterly lost—just like the hills in our town that had been cut up to provide landfill for Omaha's riverside development or to make room for a local retirement villa or for the new high school baseball field. A school where our children would undoubtedly be taught the tragedy of destroying the Amazonian rain forest.

This was how, moment to moment, the view here opened the door to awe and wonder, only to slam it shut again.

Our destination, this time, was a small lake nestled against the Loess Hills. The morning sun was still hidden behind the crests, and everything, the trees, the grass, looked wet and new. The mist, which Spencer described as "cotton candy," clung to the surface of the water and to the hillsides towering nearby, obscuring their dimensions. There was only the sense of something huge and significant and maybe alive hunkered down near the lake, watching from above.

Steph handed out the fishing poles and the bait, helping the boys secure it on their hooks. After establishing the proper spacing, we cast into the water and I prepared myself for yet another interminable stretch of silence and suffering.

Almost immediately, Steph and Spencer, who were sharing a pole, got a bite. They reeled it closer to the shore and discovered a small crappie at the end of the line. Ben giggled.

"A crappy crappie!"

"He's not crappy," Spencer yelled back. "He's Caden!"

"Great," I interjected, feeling the old revulsion. "Now let's set it free."

"Whoa there, hotshot," Steph interrupted. "We have certain rules, right boys?"

Apparently we weren't allowed to immediately release the fish. We had to use the net to gently lift it into a bucket of pond water, where it could be observed and admired up close—its spiky fins and shiny scales that changed color in the sunlight. If other children were around, it was permissible to call them over to admire the fish in the bucket as well. The boys noticed a family with kids sitting at a distant picnic table preparing their own poles. We could hear bits of Spanish floating over the water. Steph, who'd been a middle-school Spanish teacher, had been trying to teach Ben and Spencer a few words and phrases, and they clearly saw this as an opportunity to try them out.

"Hola!" they shouted, as they ran off toward the family.

They returned with two kids around their age, Victor and Elena, who seemed very interested in the "pez." They commenced conversing with Steph in Spanish, with Ben and Spencer contributing their own homemade phrases:

"No way, problema!"

"Holy tomingo!"

I would have laughed at them, but the boys probably were more advanced Spanish speakers than I'd ever be. I'd taken two years of Spanish in graduate school, and for me, each class wasn't that different from what this fish experienced when yanked from the water, only instead of gasping for oxygen, I'd gasped for words. It was mystifying. No matter how much I studied—and I studied a lot—when the instructor asked me a question in class, I could only answer: "No se, lo siento." *I'm sorry, I don't know.* It was more a plea than an apology, and it remains one of the few Spanish phrases I can readily recall. Luckily the instructor, a native Spaniard and fellow graduate student, was merciful. During the final oral exam, he asked me to describe the town of Iowa City. All I could come up with was "pequeño y blanco." *Small and white.* This was accurate in a way, but clearly more was expected. He sighed and asked me to describe the house I grew up in, and once again, I replied "pequeño y blanco." He kept dumbing down the questions—describe your car, your pet, yourself—all of which I answered in the same way: "pequeño y blanco." Finally, he pointed to the white eraser on the end of his pencil, and at last the answer adequately fit the question, allowing him to pass me.

I hoped the boys, unlike me, would learn early on to swim between languages and cultures and have friends who could do the same. Regardless, it was clear the little bit of nature swimming in the bucket was connecting these children in ways more powerful than words. The intense look in their eyes, the excitement in their voices, the bodies bent over the bucket, so close the hairs on their heads touched—all of it was enough to bridge whatever trivialities separated them.

After everyone had fully appreciated the fish, it was time to let it go. Steph granted Victor and Ben the honor of carrying the bucket to the shore and gently pouring the fish back into the lake.

"Adios," Victor said.

Ben waved: "Hasta la blistro, baby!"

If the fishing experience had ended here, we could have called it a Hallmark card and gone home, but no such luck.

After Victor and Elena returned to their family, Steph and the boys caught a number of other fish, including more crappy crappies, a bluegill, and a striped bass, all of which must have experienced some form of surprise when, after being hooked through the mouth and ogled by juvenile primates, they found themselves back in the lake, scot-free. I was feeling similarly liberated when Steph announced we'd all take one more cast before heading home. I threw my line into the shallows, thinking no fish would be there, and slowly began reeling it in.

There was a stout tug.

At first, I thought I'd snagged a log, and I yanked hard, trying to free it, but then it yanked back and actually forced me to take a step forward.

"Stephanie?"

"Oh, look, boys, your father's about to become a hypocrite."

"Funny. I think I'm going to need your help with this—it's huge!"

"That's what they all say."

She stopped joking when I handed her the line. She gave it a few pulls and raised her eyebrows.

"Keep at it," she said, handing the pole back to me. The boys gathered around as I wrestled what was clearly going to be the largest fish they'd ever seen—maybe one of those monster catfish we were always seeing photos of in the paper. It was taking longer than expected to bring it in. I could definitely feel movement at the other end, but it was slow and in the opposite direction. I couldn't help but imagine myself as Hemingway's Old Man, heroically reeling in the giant marlin, or, even better, as Hemingway himself. Or perhaps just a father to be admired. Steph and the boys were shouting encouragement—"Don't give up!"—and Victor and Elena, hearing all the excitement, returned to cheer me on.

Finally, when the line was almost directly below us and my arms were starting to cramp, Steph put the net in the water and came up with . . . *a carp.*

They all started laughing. "Dad caught a stupid bottom-feeder!" Ben exclaimed. "Carp eat other fish's garbage!" But then they realized this was a pretty cool carp. It was, as predicted, a big fish, over a foot long and covered with iridescent gold and black scales. The disco ball of carp! It was too large to fit in the bucket, so after Steph carefully removed the hook, we used the net to gently detain it in the water. The fish didn't struggle or try to escape. It just lingered there, patiently, as if it knew the routine.

Occasionally, the fish would raise the top of its head above the water and sort of look at us. It reminded me a little of a drawing in one my favorite childhood books, *The Magic Fish,* based on an old Scandinavian folk tale. The fish in that story was also sparkly, because it was a magic prince in disguise. A fisherman had caught it, but then he let it go out of respect for royalty. Later, his wife demanded he return and ask the magic fish to replace their old shack with a pretty house. The man reluctantly did so, and the fish granted the request. His wife was happy with their new home, but not for long. She sent him back to ask for a castle, and then to become "Queen of all the land." Each time the man returned to beg for something new, his shoulders became more hunched from the shame, while the sea became rougher, angrier. Still, the magic fish granted her requests. Finally, the wife demanded to be made "Queen of the sun and the moon and the stars," and so the man— nearly crawling now—returned to the sea, where the waves were boiling and crashing onto the shore, soaking the man to the bone, threatening to sweep him away. The magic fish appeared, but this time he refused to grant her wish.

"She wants too much!" he declared, and took away all the other wishes, returning them to their old hut.

When I was a kid, I knew I was supposed to be on the side of the man and the fish—I'd been told so by the grown-ups who read it to me. The hut by the sea should have been enough, they said. The wife was greedy. But part of me also understood how wishing could start small, like wanting a toy for Christmas or a bunk bed, and then, if something bad happens to your family, grow into a desire to control the sun and the moon and the stars. Which is to say everything, including time, including life and death. As a boy, I'd known what it felt like to be so close to realizing my dream of having a brother, only to lose it all and be back where I started. I'd felt the fisherman's burden in my own shoulders back then, as I, too, had taken on the wishes of others or what I thought were their wishes: to make up for the lost boy by being doubly perfect, doubly successful. The boy who would never disappoint, never fail.

The boy who would save them all, the whole world.

I'd read and reread that story, the blue cover becoming so worn and folded that the fish on the wave was, through those folds, brought closer and closer to the man. As if to answer my own wish that the growing rift between them might be healed, before it was too late and the magic went away. I could feel it even now, as I looked at the towering hills along the lake. The mist had lifted, revealing their bare erosions and excavations, the chokehold of trees and shrubs, reminding me how earth, as well as our bodies, bears the burden of our collective desires.

And yet, as I thought about that story, I couldn't help but entertain some wishing of my own. Not just for a nicer house or more money or better health insurance, but for grander things, no less real for their impossibility. To give my grandmother a different childhood and a little peace, to heal the natural world around me, to protect my children, all children, from harm. To keep my wife safe from cancer.

It went on and on, because as the story conveyed, wishing could take on a life of its own, eventually consuming everything, including any possibility of contentment.

"Can we keep the fish?" Ben asked. "I wanna show it to William."

"You know that's against the rules," Steph replied. "It probably has a family, and they would miss him if he just vanished."

She bent down and carefully removed the net from the water, leaving the fish free to swim off, except it didn't. It stayed there, as if waiting for something. I couldn't help myself.

Magic fish, I thought, *if I can put all the rest of it aside—the house, the money, the control—would it be too much to ask that my loved ones be free from fear and death?*

The fish paused a moment more, then slipped away into deeper water.

12

Praying Mantis, or How I Became Jim Fowler

SPENCER'S CRYING woke us up in the middle of the night. When we entered his room, Ben had already climbed down from the top bunk to comfort him, as he had the times before.

"It's OK," Ben was telling him. "Big Brudda is here."

We joined them, putting our arms around Spencer. He'd had another bad dream about Grandma K, he said. He'd been having a lot of them recently, and though the details were a little fuzzy, they always involved Grandma dying or Spencer dying or both of them dying together. We'd tried to reassure him the dreams weren't real, but it was a hard sell, given the situation. Usually he ended up crawling into our bed and asking us to leave the light on all night. We didn't mind. Steph and I had been having some restless nights ourselves during the last few days, waiting for the results from her biopsy. We might as well be restless together.

"What can we do to help this time, honey?" Steph asked.

"I wanna talk to Gramma K."

I wasn't sure that was a good idea, but I was willing to say anything to comfort him.

"She's asleep right now," I told him, "but how about we call her right away in the morning?"

He nodded and sniffled and laid his head back on the pillow. We stayed with him, including Ben, until he fell asleep.

I'd hoped Spencer would forget about calling Grandma, but the next morning he brought the telephone to us in bed. I reluctantly dialed her number and handed it back to him.

"Hi Gramma K," he said, when she answered. "Hi Niña."

I wanted to hover for a while to monitor the conversation, but Steph insisted we give them privacy and nudged me out the bedroom door.

Spencer was on the line a good ten minutes—probably his longest phone conversation to date. I was nervous when I heard him coming down the stairs, but he seemed in better spirits. Whatever Grandma had said to him must have worked, but I didn't want to press our luck by asking him about it.

"I'm hungry," he said. "Can we go to the Chinese buffet?"

Although it was late morning, we honored Spencer's request and headed over to the Chinese buffet in midtown Omaha. This was the boys' favorite restaurant, and had been since they were in the womb. During both pregnancies, Steph had experienced irresistible cravings for piles of fried rice and spring rolls and salty shrimp and rangoons and fake sushi and other delicacies offered at that fine establishment.

"Baby loves buffet!" became a kind of mantra for her.

The babies had now become boys, but the cravings for Chinese buffet had only intensified. On the rare occasions when we did go out to eat, it was always their first choice. During that late morning, we had the entire place to ourselves, being that most citizens of Omaha were enjoying normal breakfasts. The boys took advantage, filling their plates with mountains of food, then going back for seconds and thirds, and finishing it all off with a trip to the sundae bar. As a father, I had to admit there was something deeply satisfying about watching my offspring eat as much as they wanted, and so cheaply. Unfortunately, Steph and I followed their example— we'd had a rough week—and by the time we crawled back into the car, we were nearly catatonic. I only hoped I could make it home before passing out.

I'd just begun to pull out of the parking space when Ben shouted:

"LOOK! A BUG!"

He was pointing at something in the window of the restaurant, nearly fifteen feet away, which to me looked like an indistinct twig.

"It's not a TWIG, Dad; it's a GI-NORMOUS PRAYING MANTIS!"

Then again, this is Ben. He can spot a terror at almost any distance. With him along, no spider-web tragedy goes unnoticed ("I guess that fly wishes he'd slept in today, right Dad?"), no roadkill goes unquestioned ("I guess that deer didn't look both ways before crossing the highway, right Dad?"), no trip to the movie rental store is ever entirely benign ("I guess we won't be able to rent that movie way over there, the one with the scary man with the bloody chainsaw, right Dad?").

"So what are you WAITING for, Dad?" Ben continued. "Go and SAVE it before it gets HURT!"

"Yeah," Spencer joined in. "Go SAVE it!"

Given Spencer's recent nightmares, I had little choice—that bug could be somebody's grandma. Even if that were not the case, the window of a Chinese buffet in downtown Omaha did not appear to be ideal mantid habitat. A rescue operation seemed in order. Still, I hesitated—this was no lunky fish. This was an air-breather that might actually fight back. When I was a boy, I knew mantids only from books, movies, and my own nightmares. They'd been on a par with the mythological monsters in Ray

Harryhausen movies—the bulbous eyes, the serrated forearms and claws, poised to strike like lightning at its helpless prey. The revulsion to this insect appeared to link the generations. The conservationist Gerald Durrell wrote in the 1950s that when he was a boy, he considered mantids "the quintessence of evil":

> They were lank and green, with chinless faces and monstrous globular eyes, frosty gold, with an expression of intense, predatory madness in them. The crooked arms, with their fringes of sharp teeth, would be raised in mock supplication to the insect world, so humble, so fervent, trembling slightly when a butterfly flew too close.

You'd think Ben would have been similarly wary of mantids, given his first encounter with the species. When he was around Spencer's age, I took him to see an IMAX film at the zoo called *Bugs! A Rainforest Adventure*. The advertisement had described it as an exciting, informative film about endangered rain forest ecosystems as seen from the perspective of insects. Good for the entire family, it said. And it was 3-D! Ben and I settled into our seats at the theater, put on our glasses, and soon found ourselves lost in the lush, life-tangled tapestry of the Borneo rain forest—stereophonic monkey calls, waterfalls, swarms of butterflies that seemed to flutter from the screen into our arms. Ben reached out to touch them.

The plot alternately followed the lives and adventures of two insects: Papilio the butterfly and Hierodula the praying mantis. We watched Papilio from her early days as a caterpillar to her emergence from her chrysalis, becoming a glorious flicker of color against the mass of green. Heirodula, along with hundreds of his siblings, burst from a papery egg case and set off to eat his way through the rain forest, consuming a number of anonymous insects just inches (it seemed) from our faces. Despite my earlier prejudice against mantids, I found myself becoming emotionally attached to him, as well as to Papilio. There were near misses for both, scrapes with predators, and several exciting subplots: battling rhino beetles, a hostile spiny katydid, scorpions, tarantulas, and a colony of three million bats fluttering straight at us from off the screen.

The major emphasis, however, was on the beautiful interconnectedness of the rain forest—the "circle of life," as Ben's *Lion King* video sang it.

As the film progressed, the stories of Papilio and Heirodula became intertwined, both of them occupying the same abandoned, decrepit hut along a jungle river. I suppose I should have known what was going to happen, especially with narrator Judi Dench tossing out lines like: "You're on somebody's menu the moment you hatch." But I didn't see it coming, not even when Papilio landed on the same leaf occupied by Heirodula—what were the chances? Not even when they moved closer and closer to each other, the music rising dramatically. I didn't see it until the moment when, with a quick jerk, Heirodula snatched Papilio with his forelegs and ate her.

There was a collective gasp in the theater, including my own, and children started crying. Ben was furious.

"Get away from her!" he screamed, whacking his hand at the screen. "Get away!"

I'm not sure what I, or anyone, should have expected from a meeting of mantis and butterfly, but like Ben, I was outraged— why had there been no parental warning? Good for the entire family? This wasn't some anonymous fly in a web, this was Papilio, with whom the creators of this little horror flick had encouraged us to become emotionally involved. Now I, along with the rest of the parents, was left to deal with the aftermath. My first impulse was to comfort Ben by telling him Heirodula would soon get his head eaten off while copulating, but that might have provoked even more uncomfortable questions.

During the film's halfhearted dénouement, I recalled similar nature films I'd seen during my own boyhood in Iowa. There was one about a cougar and his mate, and though I can't remember the title, I recall that one of them fell to his or her death while escaping hunters. Even worse were those 1940s and '50s movies like *Old Yeller*, in which a boy is forced to shoot his beloved dog after it contracts rabies during a fight with a wolf. And *The Yearling*, where another boy is forced to kill the deer he'd helped raise from a fawn because it began eating the family's corn crop.

"Who cares about the stupid corn?" I bawled at the television screen as the boy walked off into the woods with his gun. For a long time afterward, I had a hard time looking at a cornfield with anything but hatred, gagging whenever my mother put a steaming, buttery cob on my plate. A major problem in Iowa.

The intended moral of *The Yearling* was the same as the other films: death is a part of nature, a part of life. At least that's how those films were explained to me by the nervous grown-ups with whom I shared my feelings and questions about them. Now, though, it seems to me that what those films were really about was teaching young boys that the first step toward becoming a man is killing what you love.

Killing your ability to love.

But it wasn't just a boy thing. One Saturday while in junior high, Stephanie was invited to the movies by a girl in her class whose older sister was dying of bone cancer. When the girl's mother picked Steph up in their car, the older sister, who had lost all of her hair, smiled at her from the front seat. At the theater, they all settled in for what appeared to be a cute, live-action film about a family of glacier foxes. At some point during the movie, however, the mother fox got caught in a trap and bled to death, leaving the father to raise the pups on his own. Then, one by one, the pups died, including the blind runt who one moment was playing near the rough seashore and the next was gone, the waves washing away its tiny paw prints in the sand.

Steph remembers them all sobbing in the theater, especially the girls' mother. Even now, Steph can't talk reasonably about this film—*abusive* is the term she uses. How was that film informative? What did it teach them that they didn't already know?

Thankfully, Ben shed no tears after the IMAX film, and though angry with Heirodula, it seemed not to have prejudiced him against mantids in general. In the parking lot of the Chinese buffet, Ben and Spencer continued to plead with me to help the mantis perched in the window. Steph even chimed in.

"What are you waiting for, *Jim*?" she chided. "Get out there and save that mantis!"

She was referring to Jim Fowler from the old *Mutual of Omaha's Wild Kingdom* television show, which ran on Sunday nights during our childhoods. On *Wild Kingdom*, any problem could be fixed if you had a muscular white man, a large net, a tranquilizer gun, and a helicopter. The episodes, hosted by silver-haired Marlin Perkins and his pencil mustache, took place all over the world but inevitably included moving the featured animal to "more ideal habitat," which, to my way of thinking back then, meant it would never again be hunted, never be in danger or know pain or fear. The image of various kinds of legs and tails sticking out from a net or a cage, then going airborne into a sunset, is probably one of my earliest impressions of mercy.

So I retrieved a crumpled sandwich baggie from beneath my seat and stepped out of the car. As I approached the mantis, which Spencer had already named "Penny," I noticed she was much larger than expected, perhaps six inches, and not at all friendly looking. I retreated to the car (enduring a number of jeers) to grab a pencil, which I could use to guide her into the bag. Penny was having none of it. She reared up and snapped at the pencil with her big spiny forelegs. There I was, just like Jim with his rippling, tan muscles and big net, facing down the giant anaconda or lion or crocodile, except I was a skinny middle-aged man with a pencil and a sandwich baggie. Ben was Marlin Perkins, narrating and shouting out instructions from the safety of the helicopter.

"Watch out, Dad, she could bite! There you go . . . get her . . . *ooh* . . . don't let her escape, Dad! Dad, don't let her . . . *ooh* . . . JUST GET HER IN THE BAG, DAD!"

Which I finally did, and, mission accomplished, we transported the mantis to a more ideal habitat: our backyard. I knew from my last experience capturing an animal in the wild, the giant Iowa carp, that it was against "the rules" to release it right away. So I let Ben and Spencer take turns holding the bag to look at her up close. Penny took a couple of snaps at both of them—she was truly ferocious—and I experienced a moment of sympathy for all the unsuspecting bugs in our yard, including the resident Heirodula who would make the mistake of falling for her deadly charm. We finally let her out onto a rhubarb leaf (another dangerous thing) near the lilac bushes. She continued to face us down, swaying back and forth, poised to strike. As we stepped away, we looked back one more time to see the green slice of her body move off the leaf and disappear. It would be the last we saw of Penny, but when winter came, we'd find a number of empty egg sacs in the overgrown, jungly areas of the yard.

Later that evening, we read stories to the boys on the couch, then went upstairs for bedtime. Big Brudda Ben crawled into the lower bunk, next to Spencer, "to protect him from any more nightmares." After we tucked them in, they folded their hands and began their nightly prayer, the children's prayer: *Now I lay me down to sleep, I pray the Lord my soul to keep. Guide me through the starry night and wake me up in the morning light. Amen.* This was the modern, toned-down version, which they'd learned from a musical book of prayers Gramma K had given them. This version replaced the final line that had haunted me and so many other children from my generation and earlier: *If I should die before I wake, I pray the Lord my soul to take.*

Remembering that lost line made me think of prairie nights during previous decades and centuries when children (and their parents) did in fact die in their sleep, in droves, of disease and cold and other deprivations. Their tombstones filled the small pioneer cemeteries dotting the rural midwestern landscapes, hidden among patches of prairie grasses and wildflowers, a remnant of the land as it was then, when it claimed them—as wild and beautiful and dangerous as the rain forest.

There were still dangers here, anywhere, but who wanted to think of them?

Ben did.

"Please, God," he said, hands still crossed under his chin, eyes staring through the ceiling, "take care of Penny and help her find lots to eat and don't let anything hurt her."

Outside in the yard, beyond sight, was the answer. Not quite the spirit of mercy that inspired Ben's prayer, but a prayer nonetheless.

Forearms crossed, eyes on the promising darkness.

13

Metamorphosis

JUNE IS TADPOLE TIME. That year, the boys named their tadpoles Critter and Leif, which they'd found, as usual, in a pond near the Missouri River. The pond was bordered by flower-filled meadows, a small restored prairie, and groves of cottonwoods that released a marzipan scent when warmed by the spring sun. Hundreds of frogs made their music there. Whenever we walked along the shore, they jumped into the water, plunking like single notes on an old piano.

The music of frogs may not be long for this world. Their permeable skin makes them vulnerable to poisons in the water, and amphibian populations have dropped precipitously all over the globe. The boys were trying to do their part by collecting two pollywogs each summer, raising them safely to frogness, and then returning them to the pond, their home. Perhaps they were helping, but who knew for sure?

What we did know was that Ben and Spencer thought the metamorphosis of tadpole into frog was very cool, and so did we—from the first leg buds to the shrinking tail to the morning when we came downstairs to find them perched on a rock, breathing free air. The idea that such wholesale transformation was possible suggested, as it always had, that there was still some magic left in the world. They were like those mythic figures in Ovid's *Metamorphoses,* becoming a flower or a spider or a heifer. As my Classics professor pointed out, however, no matter how much those characters changed on the outside, their inner natures, their dreams and desires, remained the same.

I wondered if that was true for the frogs. Even after their tadpole gills, like scars, disappeared, they still spent all their time in or near the water. I knew the biological reasons for this. What I wanted to know was how much they longed, inside, to return completely to their origins.

Critter and Leif were just sprouting legs when we returned to Fort Dodge for the annual Price family reunion. It had been bundled with my (early) fortieth birthday party to save everyone time and expense. That was fine by me. I didn't want a party, but Steph insisted it was a milestone worth celebrating. Given recent events, I couldn't really argue.

We'd shown up at the doctor's office together, as scheduled, to receive the results of Steph's biopsy. It hadn't been a week since our last visit, but it felt like years. We sat in the lobby with the other patients, almost completely silent, thumbing through magazines in the hopes of forgetting why we were there. When the doctor finally called us into her office, she put her arm around Steph.

"You're clear," she said.

Steph broke down, and so did I.

After we pulled ourselves together, the doctor explained that this was a wake-up call (I'd heard that phrase a lot recently) to get serious about testing. With Steph's dense breast tissue, mammograms wouldn't be enough; she would need an MRI as soon as possible and then one every other year, at least. That seemed reasonable, but at some point during the discussion, it hit me that this wasn't going away. When it came to breast cancer, the rest of her years—our years—would be lived with a baseline of fear.

Not long after the doctor's visit, my mother called to say Aunt Esther was dying. At that moment, she was unconscious and Mom and Dad were sitting at her bedside at the care facility, holding her hand and waiting for the inevitable. I'd been very close to Esther, but her mind had declined over the years, until it seemed the person I knew had already moved on. My children never had the chance to really know her. While on the phone with my mother, the memories came rushing back, especially those winter afternoons during my adolescence when I'd visited Esther's home in the small town of Boone, Iowa. Her husband, Leonard, had died in 1975, and they had no children, though she treated us like her own. With the distant sound of trains and church chimes in the background, I'd lose the hours (and my teenage angst) learning from her how to paint landscapes in oils, listening to stories of my immigrant Swedish ancestors, singing Swedish folk tunes, learning bits of the language, eating potato sausages with lingonberries, and watching *Perry Mason* reruns.

As an accomplished artist, Esther tried to teach me how to see the world around us, its every detail, as a thing of beauty, waiting to be transformed by brush or pencil into a gift for those we love. Which, for the artist, should include everyone. A number of those gifts were hanging in frames on the walls of our home. In that sense, it wasn't quite accurate to say my children didn't know Esther. Every time they stopped to admire her paintings, every time they took in that autumn oak, that morning glory vine, that gold-and-lavender iris, that prairie stream, they experienced the world through Esther's attentive, affectionate eyes.

"Could you please put the phone up to Esther's ear?" I asked my mother.

"Sure," she said, "but I don't know if she's aware of anything."

I could hear my aunt's shallow breaths get a little louder.

"Tack så mycket, Esther," I said, as she had taught me. "Jag älskar dig."

Thanks so much. I love you.

Esther slipped away later that evening. My parents decided to hold the funeral the Monday following the family reunion/fortieth birthday party, when everyone was still home. If Esther were alive, I think she would've found humor in the juxtaposition, but I didn't. I'd had my fill of mortality for one season.

My sisters and their families attended the reunion, as did my father's brother Denny and his entire family, with whom we'd always been close. During the half hour dedicated to my personal "milestone," they showered me with gifts and cards, many of which made me laugh—I hadn't known how much I needed that. Steph created a nice display of photographs from my life, including one of me and my cousin Steve (who was in attendance) wearing curlers and our mothers' nighties. There was another photo of me at high school graduation, standing between Grandma Kathryn and Grandpa Andy. Despite his difficulty walking, Grandpa had insisted on making the trip from Arizona for the event. That had meant a lot to me. There were also many pictures of me with the boys, emphasizing the sometimes surreal fact that I am a father.

"Open our presents, Dad!" Ben said, handing me two hand-wrapped packages, mummified with Scotch tape. The first was a Dracula action figure, complete with flying bat and soil-filled crypt. No secret who that was from. The second was an old man doll about the size of Baby, with a T-shirt reading "Life Begins at 40."

Did it? I wondered. Would this otherwise random marker of change hearken in a new, positive era in my life?

If the end of the party was any indication of that new life, I had reason to worry. I don't know if it was the intensity of the last few weeks—the entire spring, for that matter—or just getting caught up in socializing with my cousins, but I consumed way too much beer and barbecue chicken and cake. So much that during the traditional family performance of the Village People's "YMCA," somewhere between the C and the A, I had to excuse myself to go vomit.

"Sorry I missed your party," Grandma said the next day when I visited her at Friendship Haven. "I wasn't feeling well."

She was sitting on the couch, with Niña eyeballing me from her lap. Grandma appeared considerably weaker, but there was something else different about her, something larger. I couldn't explain it.

"That's OK, Grandma," I said. "I wasn't feeling very good myself."

"That's too bad," she said. "Hey, before I forget, I want you to have this."

She took a small, leather-bound volume off the coffee table and handed it to me. It had a locked metal clasp, with a tiny key taped to the back of the cover.

"This is my high school diary. As the family historian, I thought you might find it interesting, but you must promise not to read it until after I'm gone. I'm not sure you'll recognize the person I was back then."

"I promise," I said, but couldn't help wondering what secrets were contained on its pages.

"Now I want you to take me for a little drive."

Grandma had a hard time walking, so I brought her out to the car in a wheelchair. As I helped her into the front seat, she felt very light in my arms, hardly there.

"Where to?" I asked.

"Lehigh."

I thought she was joking. Did she really want me to take her to her childhood home? If so, this was going to be a much longer journey than expected, geographically and emotionally. I assumed that while revisiting the places where she'd lived as a young girl, she'd also be revisiting all the negative experiences and feelings associated with that period in her life.

As it turned out, it was a different kind of journey altogether.

The surprises began as we turned south off the Fort Dodge business strip and headed into the country. Grandma reached over and took my hand.

"I want you to know, John, that my vet has decided to adopt Niña, which makes me so happy I could cry. No one needs to worry about that anymore. I'm sorry for the pressure I put on you about that, and for some of the things I said about my family."

"That's OK."

"No, it's not, but I'm glad you're with me today. I have some places I need to see and I want you to see them too."

The road passed a few miles of crop fields and gypsum pits, then took a steep dive into the Des Moines River Valley. After ascending the other side, Grandma asked me to park near an old white church. This was a familiar spot to me. When I was a teenager, I used to take long bicycle rides on this road with my father. They had been a good opportunity for us to spend time together, during a stretch when his midlife work and worries, like mine now, must have threatened to draw his attention elsewhere. At the top of that killer hill, we would get off the bikes, sip from our water bottles, and reward ourselves with one of the most spectacular views of the surrounding countryside and river valley. I'd spent much of my youth thinking my home landscape was ordinary, but up here my father had offered me an experience of its beauty to get lost in. Which also meant it had been too easily forgotten.

Grandma had different memories.

"Your grandfather and I used to park right here to do some necking. We were just dating then, but I suppose I fell a little in love with him up here. I had a lot of boys after me—Sheik and Whitey and Hutch—and I necked with a few of them, as you'll discover in the journal, but there was just something about Andy."

"Do I want to know what that 'something' was?"

"Oh, don't be so filthy. I'm talking about *love*, John. I was barely fifteen when I first saw your grandfather. I was serving ice cream at the Fort Konza swimming pool when he drove up in that sporty Ford with his leg hanging over the side. He was so dreamy and so much fun, and I needed that in my life, even after we were married. You remember that story I told about his rowdy friends at our first apartment? Well, there was this lady next door who was always complaining about the noise and making my life miserable. So one night Andy and his buddies stuck raw wieners out of their zippers, knocked on her door, and when she peeked out they cut the wieners off with kitchen knives!"

Grandma burst into laughter.

"Anyway," she said, catching her breath, "we used to romance up here. Whenever we drove past, we'd smile at each other. I thought you'd like to know that."

"Thanks," I said.

"Well, I hate to break it to you, John, but you weren't made by tossing a coin in a cabbage patch."

Mercifully, we started back down the road, where Grandma asked to take a short detour toward the small town of Otho. Its grain elevator and blue water tower were just visible above the fields. On the eastern edge of town, at a broad turn in the road, she told me to pull onto the gravel shoulder.

"This was Grandpa and Grandma Porter's home," she said, pointing to a small, square house. "This was where they moved after they lost the farm in Lehigh and all the land. That western bedroom is where my grandfather J. W. died."

They got most of their water out of an old well pump, she recalled, which was still there. The house didn't have any indoor plumbing, so they had to go in a porcelain pot, which they kept under the bed. The only other option was the ramshackle outhouse, which wasn't really an option during subzero winter nights. Even now, the place seemed exposed, with only a few scraggly maples to protect it from the wind coming off the fields.

"Is that a garden in the backyard?" she asked, leaning forward. "Grandpa always had a huge garden. After he died, all his mail order seeds arrived and there was no way Grandma could plant them. So Andy, bless his heart, planted them for her, but instead of staggering them across a few weeks, he planted them all at once. All those vegetables came in at the same time! He had to come out here every other day to harvest them, but he made sure Grandma was fully stocked, and us, and then he delivered a bunch to a poor family we knew who had six children to feed. The daughter, who was a little girl at the time, told me later that her mother canned enough of those vegetables to get them through the entire fall and winter."

"Your grandfather could be a lot of fun," she continued, looking me straight in the eyes, "and he could be frustrating, but I want you to remember there was this other side of him too. He was always helping others. We went together almost five years before we got married, because his folks had no income except what Andy gave them. That's a big reason why he didn't go to college. That's no small thing, to give everything you have to your loved ones, to sacrifice your own dreams. It took a toll on him as well, but it made me love him all the more. That part of him never changed. When our finances were low, he wouldn't buy a thing for himself, not even a drink. He never abandoned us, like my father did. We had rough times in our marriage, like everyone, and I'm not white-washing his struggles with alcohol, but overall he was a good father and husband. A good person."

"You're a pretty good person yourself."

"I haven't always thought so. You know, this house is where I promised my dying grandfather I'd take care of Grandma Josie. I thought I'd failed him, but now that I'm out here, I remember how Mother sometimes would telephone me in the middle of the night, when Grandma was having one of her violent fits, and I'd drive all the way down here and sing Grandma a nursery rhyme to calm her. Then I'd tuck her in bed and manicure her nails, and she'd look up at me with such tenderness in her eyes. There were a lot of moments like that between us."

She took another long look at the house.

"So, I don't know, maybe I did keep my promise."

Lehigh is nestled so deep in the Des Moines River Valley that when you first descend into it from the surrounding fields and woods, it feels as if you're falling into the earth. It was originally a coal mining town, named for the Lehigh Valley in Pennsylvania, and it also had a thriving clay works factory. Both industries tapped out decades ago. It was a fairly populous town at the turn of the century, but it now had less than five hundred residents, many of them older. The rough wood and brick buildings along the main street, some of them empty, had clearly seen better days.

The Lehigh my grandmother recalled, however, was riding the high crest of prosperity, as was her family. We drove by the locations of her grandfather's theater and his meat market and butcher shop, and the Masonic Temple he'd bankrolled. She remembered a number of bustling stores along the main street, including a soda fountain where she'd tried her first Coca-Cola with her cousin Kathleen.

"It was awful," she said. "I think I spit it out."

"Speaking of spitting," I said, "was it somewhere along here that the miners spit on your Grandma Josie?"

"Probably, but you know, Lehigh was always a tough town."

She revealed that when Esther learned her little brother Andy was dating a "Lehigh girl," she'd worried for his immortal soul. The town's reputation hadn't changed much in my time, but like people, it had other sides to appreciate. I would discover later that when Grandma's father, Clifford Hobson, was playing ball in Lehigh, the local team paid John Donaldson, one of the great African American pitchers, a fairly substantial sum to throw for them. This was during a stretch when many towns refused to play Negro teams or worse. That interracial Lehigh Sewer Pipe & Tile Company team, on which my great-grandfather played second base, went on to defeat the "big city" team of Fort Dodge and many others.

Donaldson was eventually hired as a scout for the Chicago White Sox, but fondly referred to Lehigh as "home."

What truly defined Lehigh, however, was the river, which flowed through the middle of town. The Des Moines is the largest river in the state, running 525 miles from its headwaters in Minnesota to meet the Mississippi in the old steamboat town of Keokuk. The origin of the name "Des Moines" is still debated. I'd been taught it was from the French for "the monks," but it could have also been derived from various words meaning "the mounds," "from the middle," or "the lesser." The more likely source is an American Indian word—and perhaps a practical joke. In 1673, when Jacques Marquette encountered representatives of the Peoria tribe near the river's confluence with the Mississippi, he asked for the name of another tribe living upstream. Recognizing a potential trade rival with the French, the Peoria responded that the tribe in question was called the "Moingona." White traders interpreted this as something like "people of the mounds," but according to one scholar of the Miami-Illinois language, it actually meant "shit-faced people." It is now the name of our capital city.

What isn't debatable is that the Des Moines River Valley is one of the most beautiful places in Iowa. Since bursting through the retreating edge of a glacier more than eleven thousand years ago, the river has scoured out a deep entrenchment, two hundred feet in some places, with dramatic terraces and stone outcroppings and canyons and caves. Over the millennia, its bordering forests, prairies, and wetlands have been home to countless wildlife as well as communities of ancient people. Burial mounds and petroglyphs can still be found there. Whatever the origin of its name, the Des Moines has long been a place of story, of community, of life. It was also the river of my grandmother's youth, and my own. All of our favorite natural areas, including nearby Dolliver State Park, were in some way graced by its waters.

As we meandered up and down the slopes of Lehigh, taking in one view of the river after another, Grandma shared memories of ice skating, wading, fishing, and exploring its banks as a young girl. It was in orientation to the river that she finally located the street on which she'd lived with her grandparents. It ran up yet another dramatic slope, and about halfway she told me to stop in front of a broken-down two-story. This had been her grandparents' "Victorian house on the hill," she said, or at least what was left of it. Spruce trees grew hard against the front, but they couldn't hide the flaking brown paint, the boarded-up windows, and busted siding. Grandma remembered there being houses on either side, but they'd since been torn down or maybe fallen down. Her grandparents' house appeared to be leaning as well, and I assumed it was abandoned until I heard a dog barking inside.

"This used to be a wonderful home," she said. "Not just how it looked, but all the laughter and joy that happened here. Grandma and Grandpa were always teasing each other and having fun, and it rubbed off on us when we first came here from Chicago. Even after my grandparents lost everything and were living in that tiny place in Otho, they were happy and affectionate with each other."

Grandma turned her attention from the dilapidated house to a concrete drainage gutter running along the sidewalk. She and her little sister and their childhood friends used to play there.

"After a rain, we'd wade in it and get clay from the hillside to build dams and sail stick boats. It doesn't take much with kids, does it?"

She said they used to sled down that big hill in the winter, all the way to the river, where her grandfather would be waiting to haul them back up again. I turned the car around and followed the route of her childhood sled, down past the old Methodist church where she'd memorized Bible verses and received awards for it in Sunday school. That church had been a second home to her, she said, as the minister and his family took her and her sister, Virginia, under their wing when they first arrived from Chicago. Their kindness had become part of the bedrock of her faith.

"There have been times in my life when I've nearly lost my faith," she said, "but I always had the feeling God would answer my prayers. I think that's due in part to this church and its people, and the way they helped us when we were so scared and alone as a family. They were true Christians."

On the other side of town, we drove up another steep hillside and into the open fields, fully exposed in the afternoon sun. A mile or so down the road, she pointed out the entrance to what used to be her grandparents' farm. When we turned onto the gravel driveway, Grandma instantly recognized the large white house with the front porch, as well as the small shed that used to be a milkhouse. The old wood barn towered in back, though most of its roof had fallen in. She said she never liked spending time in that barn or with the cattle and pigs, but she fondly recalled the tree house her grandfather built in a nearby burr oak and the "lake" that always formed beneath the windmill after a big rain. The windmill was gone, but the old pump was still there.

"Sometimes the lake got so big it made my little sister seasick when she waded in it," she laughed. "One time she was so dizzy Grandpa had to go in and rescue her. Virginia could be so cute sometimes. I wish she were here to see this with me."

It was the land around the farm that evoked the clearest memories. There was a nearby overgrown pioneer cemetery where she'd played hide-and-seek with her friends and read the dates on the gravestones, many of them from pioneer days, including children. There had also been a pasture full of prairie grasses and wildflowers, which her grandfather refused to plow, and a meadow where they'd played "pum-pum pullaway," and a pond where they'd swum and collected fireflies and frogs. She pointed to a wooded area where she claimed Indian mounds were hidden.

"I spent a lot of time out here feeling lonely and sorry for myself," she said, "but in many ways it was a wonderful place for a child. Being here, I can't help but think of my mother. She was so young when my father left her alone to raise two daughters. Coming back to her hometown and being part of this prominent family—it was a very public failure, I imagine. And then having to leave us out here every week to work in Fort Dodge. It must have been as hard for her as it was for me. But when I look around here, remembering how it used to be, I wonder if my mother knew I'd find some comfort growing up in such a beautiful place. Andy loved it out here too. When we were young, we would spend hours collecting wildflowers and walnuts and hazelnuts and butternuts, and horsing around over there in the woods and the meadow. I love to remember him that way. And me."

She paused to take it all in, one more time.

"This is home."

Before returning to Friendship Haven, Grandma requested we make one last stop in Fort Dodge. The little gray house on Haskell Street, where my grandfather was raised, was also located in the Des Moines River Valley. It flowed through Fort Dodge, just as it did Lehigh, though this was one of the more industrialized areas of the city. To the west, busy Hawkeye Bridge ran over Soldier Creek, while just across the street, to the north, you could make out the giant imprints of the creosote tanks that used to be there. I couldn't imagine what it must have smelled like growing up there.

This area was about as different from a farm as you could get, but it wasn't without its wild places. Aunt Esther had told me that when she and her little brother Andy were kids they would walk in the woods with their father, along the creek and river, collecting gooseberries and walnuts and picking wildflowers for their mother. Sometimes their father would sit on the edge of the river and sing songs to them in Swedish. As children, they'd learned to love nature while exploring this ancient valley, just as we had.

Aunt Esther and Grandpa Andy's parents, the Andersons, were Swedish immigrants. Tillie was a seamstress and John, my namesake, was a coopersmith who made butter tubs in a factory just a couple blocks away. They were very kind to my grandmother, she said, particularly during that difficult stretch when she was living in the Warden Apartments with her mother and stepfather. John especially liked her, and, during her occasional breakups with Andy, wouldn't let his son bring any other woman into their house. Years later, on the day John died from tuberculosis, she swore he visited her to say good-bye.

"I can't explain it," she said. "I just felt him there, beside me. When Andy came home to tell me his father was gone, I told him I already knew. It was one of the few times I saw him cry."

As a teenager, Grandma walked to the Anderson home almost every week for home-cooked meals, a relief from the café food she and her mother mostly ate while living downtown. Still, she was nervous when she brought Nina there for the first time.

"I remember taking Mother around the house and saying, 'Oh look at the lovely radio Andy bought for his parents, look at the lovely piano Esther has,' and so on. When we got home Mother said, 'Kathryn, you don't have to sell me on Andy by the things they have in their home. It's a humble home, it's a happy home, and there's love in it.' That took a lot for my mother to say, I think, since she was never quite able to re-create that in her own life, no matter who she married. She knew it wasn't easy, and it isn't. Not even for the Andersons. You knew they lost a child, didn't you?"

I nodded. Linnea, their eldest, was one year old when she reached onto the stove and tipped a kettle of boiling water on herself. The doctors covered her scalded body in a cotton wrap and accidentally suffocated her.

"Tillie and John were so grief-stricken—I know because they talked about it openly. They even had a picture of her little casket, covered in flowers, prominently displayed on a table. People didn't hide death back then."

She took my hand again.

"That reminds me of something I've been meaning to tell you, John."

It was about James. After he died, my parents didn't let anyone see his body, and none of us kids were allowed to attend the funeral. Grandma respected their grief, she said, but at the same time, she felt a strong need to see the baby. His death brought back all the memories of when her nephew Billy died and other emotions she couldn't quite understand or control. She was falling apart again. The mortician was a friend, so one night she asked him if she could spend just a few minutes holding her grandson, and he let her.

"I can still see his face and. . . ." Her voice caught. "All I know is that Billy dying was one of those times when I almost lost my faith in God. But when I saw James, I experienced something else, something I've been going back to a lot recently. He was so beautiful, John, and remembering him, I'm not afraid to die. I don't want to experience a lot of pain, but if death brings the kind of peace I saw in his face, then I'm OK with it. I think that's what Jesus meant when he said we'll enter heaven as a child—it's who we are, inside, no matter how old we get or how many mistakes we make. Knowing that makes it easier to forgive yourself and others."

"I've been wondering a lot about my father," she continued, fishing around in her purse for a tissue. "I've been so angry with him, for so long, but think how young he and Mother were— nearly children themselves—and how scared he must have been. It takes a lot of strength to raise a family, and he just wasn't strong enough. We never forgave him for leaving, and if what my grandmother Hobson said in her letter was true, I don't think he forgave himself. Why else would he go around showing off those pictures of us and his granddaughters? But when I consider all I would have missed if I'd never been born, I'm almost grateful to him. James never had that chance, and Billy and Linnea barely did. My parents' so-called mistake made all the difference and set me on this wonderful adventure, and you, too. I wouldn't take any of it back for a second."

She got quiet, and I thought she was done, but she had one more surprise.

"I know Stephanie wants another baby."

"What? How do you know that?"

"She told me, dummy. Do you think you're the only one I talk to around here?"

"No, but—"

"I can't tell you what to do," she said, "but whatever you decide, fear shouldn't decide it for you. Everyone has experienced loss, and whatever that loss is, you do your best to fill the space left behind with love and faith. That's what the Andersons did, and what your parents did, after James—they had your sister Allyson a year later. Can you imagine the world without her? You're doing the same thing every day with those two beautiful boys of yours. Don't let fear and bitterness fill that space. I know what that can do to a person. Let your love for your family and for God and for this world guide everything you do."

I didn't know what to say.

"I won't force you to make any promises, like my grandfather did, but I'll make you a promise: If you live your life with this love, it will come back around to you. All of it."

That evening, Ben and Spencer and their cousins came over to visit Grandma K at Friendship Haven. They raided the Tootsie Roll drawer, played with Niña, and ran through the other rituals—the parakeets, the popcorn machine, the lonely woman across the hall who worried about everyone's soul. Later, Grandma watched them go swimming from her wheelchair, laughing and clapping whenever they called her attention to an underwater handstand or somersault or in Spencer's case just having the courage to put his face underwater.

Back in her apartment, they dried off with the same blue-and-green paisley towels I remembered using as a boy at Grandma's house. Spencer cuddled next to her on the couch, and she kissed his head. There were more hugs and kisses, and then it was time for the kids to go back to my parents' house to be tucked into bed.

"Good-bye, my sweethearts," Grandma said, waving, as I herded them out the door. "I love you."

"Bye, Gramma K!" they all yelled. "Love you, too!"

By the time I returned to Friendship Haven, Grandma was in her bed, surrounded by my sisters. The only illumination was the dim nightlight near her bedside. My grandmother looked so beautiful.

Glowing. I could smell the gardenia skin cream Allyson had rubbed on her arms. Carrie Anne and Susan were doing her nails, which reminded me of what she used to do for her own dying grandmother. Grandma knew it too.

"You see?" she said to me, the tenderness in her eyes.

14

Flight of the Hummingbird

THERE IS A SPOT in Sabino Canyon where I used to go with my grandmother, down along the rocky creek, where hummingbirds zip and dart among the willows. She first took me to Sabino during a visit when I was fourteen or so because I told her I'd always wanted to see a canyon, and it was only half an hour from their home in Green Valley, Arizona. The fact that it was on the edge of Tucson, where the rest of my family had decided to go shopping, did nothing to alter my impression of it as "wilderness." The towering, cathedral cliffs and stately saguaro and giant boulders—the hugeness of it all—was impressive. All the more so because I was a small and awkward teenager. Time even seemed bigger in Sabino. Our guide told stories about ancient geologic formations and catastrophic earthquakes and how the giant boulders surrounding us had been pulled into the earth, remade over millennia, then reborn onto the surface. This geologic history presented a transformative possibility that, despite its violent origins, filled me with hope.

There came a point during that first tour, however, when all the immensity became a bit dizzying—or maybe I just hadn't been drinking enough water. That's when Grandma spotted the quiet grove of willows along the Sabino Dam Trail, where someone had hung a few hummingbird feeders. We sat at an old concrete picnic table and watched the tiny birds flit around, their iridescent feathers—ruby, turquoise, emerald—catching the sun, sparkling.

They were themselves sparks, it seemed, shooting off the branches, hovering near the flame of a blossom or feeder for a second or two, then disappearing.

This memory returned to me while visiting Hummingbird Canyon, inside the Desert Dome at Omaha's Henry Doorly Zoo. It is the largest glazed geodesic dome in the world, 137 feet from top to bottom, and at night it can be seen from our bedroom window across the Missouri River, miles away. Inside, visitors meander among the flora and fauna of three desert environments: Africa's Namib Desert, Australia's Red Center, and North America's Sonoran Desert. It has a thirty-foot sand dune and a fifty-five-foot "mountain." Hummingbird Canyon is located near the end of the Sonoran area, an optional side trail many don't take. Its tall walls are not formed from the rise of ancient rock, as at Sabino, but from concrete molds made to look like rocks—not a canyon but the thought of a canyon, given substance.

I've read somewhere that hummingbirds are known to migrate more than two thousand miles. These particular birds, however, reside in tiny grottoes along the narrow trail, enclosed by almost invisible nets. Sometimes it is difficult to see them among the willowy branches and shadowed outcroppings. With patience, though, they can usually be spotted on the higher perches, near where the rock walls open into the dome's upper reaches. Sometimes, but not very often, they fly around.

The boys were not beside me in Hummingbird Canyon that day, though I could hear them and their cousins Tyler and Christopher on the other side of the wall, giving Steph trouble. Steph's sister

Amy, her husband, Scott, and their two boys were visiting us from Idaho, and we thought they'd enjoy touring the zoo. The Desert Dome had never been the most popular choice with the kids, however. Who needs sand and hummingbirds when, just below our feet, in the subterranean Kingdoms of the Night exhibit—the place they wanted to be—there was a towering cave full of bats and a dank swamp full of alligators and a dead-limbed terrain full of giant aardvarks and fossas? The boys were big on fossas, thanks to the movie *Madagascar,* ranking them right up there with the zoo's more traditional megafauna, including gorillas, elephants, polar bears, and rhinos. Not to mention the penguins, sea lions, sharks, giraffes, and (Ben's favorite) the red-kneed Mexican tarantula.

Less inspiring, but still popular with the boys, was the farm-themed petting zoo with its pack of crazed pygmy goats and army of hand sanitizer dispensers guarding the entrance and exit. The danger of catching E. coli from touching one of these animals—a risk that had been pointed out to our children many times by concerned adults—only made the touching more irresistible. Usually by the time we left that place, the boys' hands, sticky from snow cones and lemonade, were covered with goat hair.

I first visited Henry Doorly Zoo almost a decade before, in the winter of 1998, while interviewing for my current teaching job at the University of Nebraska at Omaha. As part of the on-campus visit, one of my future colleagues, Maria, a volunteer at the zoo, had arranged a tour of the enclosed rain forest. She and the search committee thought that since I was a nature writer, I would enjoy hanging out with some actual nature. At first I was a little disappointed—I'd hoped to visit the Loess Hills, just across the Missouri River. I'd heard how the majority of native Iowa prairie could be found there, and though I grew up just a few hours away, I'd rarely seen any of it. The possibility of settling near those magnificent hills, so close to home, was one of the main reasons I was interested in the job.

Even so, a rain forest, even a fake one, had its appeal on a freezing January day. Maria filled me in on zoo facts and history: Formally established in 1963, Henry Doorly Zoo was famous world-wide, and even Jim Fowler—Mr. Danger himself—still made the occasional appearance there. We were currently standing inside one of the largest indoor rain forests in the world, she said, with a height equivalent to an eight-story building. The trails snaked through habitats from three different continents and included towering waterfalls and damp caves and thick, authentic jungle foliage. Maria encouraged me to explore it on my own, and since it was almost closing time, I was virtually alone—unless you counted the monkeys and macaws and Malayan tapirs and pygmy hippos and vampire bats and hundreds of other creatures residing there.

I should have appreciated it more, but I was a stressed-out wreck, contemplating the interview, contemplating my professional future. In such a state, monkey screams can be hard on the nerves. So I retreated to the buttress of a giant fake tree within a private grove of ferns, where a bench had been cleverly hidden. As I practiced my presentation, I was approached by a black-green, chickenlike jungle bird that looked at me curiously and moved on. I got up and followed it along the creek, admiring the colorful orchids and minnows and freshwater stingrays gliding gracefully beneath a wooden footbridge—all of which put me in a different place, one that allowed me to set aside thoughts about the job and consider another kind of future. One that could include taking my future children to that zoo.

Since landing the job and moving to the area, Steph and I had become regular visitors, especially after Ben was born two years later, and then Spencer two years after that. We'd watched some of these creatures grow up along with our own children—including baby gorillas and orangutans—and shared some memorable adventures: the emu that attacked Ben's shirt collar while posing for a family picture, the Red Power Ranger that fell (or was pushed by Baby?) into a koi feeding frenzy, the pygmy goat that crawled into Ben's stroller and refused to get out, and the free-roaming peacocks whose screeching once startled Spencer and me so badly we dropped our ice-cream cones onto the asphalt.

The greatest adventure of all, however, had been the countless moments of awe and wonder our children had encountered in the presence of just this little bit of wild diversity. I knew the arguments against zoos, and I agreed with some of them. Henry Doorly had its imperfections as well, but was trying to correct them. For a long time, the primate area was too small and enclosed. They'd since built a three-acre facility, including an outdoor "valley" for the gorillas, with grass and trees and pools, and for the orangutans, two sixty-five-foot fake banyan trees with climbing vines, offering them intellectual as well as physical stimulation.

It still wasn't ideal, I knew. None of it was. But I also knew that the day Spencer first put his hand against the glass and a young gorilla did the same, something shifted inside him, toward the gorilla, toward all living creatures. He'd remained there ever since.

That was the first thing Spencer always did when we visited Gorilla Valley. He marched right up and put his hand against the glass, hoping one of the gorillas would return the gesture. He'd been disappointed during our last visit when none of them showed interest. They'd appeared preoccupied instead with the mood of Motuba, the giant silverback. Motuba—or "Tubby"—hadn't seemed particularly agitated that day, reclining against a tree trunk, nonchalantly picking at the grass and staring down the younger males. He was magnificent, over four hundred pounds of muscle and shimmering fur, with a noble brow that, along with his piercing eyes, projected his superiority over all the other apes, including those of us on the opposite side of the glass.

"Daddy, tell me how the gorilla is my brudda," Spencer requested, wanting to have the evolution conversation again.

"*I'm* your brudda!" Ben interjected, right on cue. Unlike Spencer, Ben had never really embraced the fact of evolution. He accepted the possibility of werewolves, even liked the idea of becoming one, but ape-human combos were another thing altogether. It's like it was beneath his dignity or something.

"Ben, you know that's not what Spencer meant," I replied. "He's talking about evolution, which, whether you like it or not, is a reality. Just look at Tubby's hands—aren't they a lot like ours? And those eyes?"

"I don't look like Tubby. I don't have black hair."

"OK, but. . . ."

"And my nose holes aren't that big."

"Yes," Steph jumped in, "but you have to admit, Ben, that his nose does resemble ours a little. And look at his facial expressions and body language. You can almost tell what kind of mood he's in, like you can with humans. Just watch him for a while and you'll see."

"I'm not fat."

"Just *watch* him."

We paused to watch Motuba. As if he read our thoughts, he turned his face and held us in his impressive gaze. I wondered then if he felt it too—the recognition, the undeniable connection. The great silverback blinked, shifted his body to the side, and I thought he might be getting ready to come over and place his huge, familiar hand on the glass in front of the boys. Instead, he slowly, deliberately reached that hand behind his haunch and pulled out a ball of poop. Holding it before his face, he studied it for a moment, then took a nibble.

"I DON'T EAT MY POOP!" Ben shouted, causing everyone to turn their heads. Kids darted over to the glass, and there was a small explosion of giggles and gasps.

"We don't eat our poop," Ben repeated to the girl next to him, and she nodded as if she completely understood. As if her father had fed her the same bull about being related to apes. Ben glared at me, defiant.

I was tempted in that moment to publicly announce that Ben had, in fact, eaten his own poop—and more than once. When he was just a toddler, he developed a habit of reaching into his diaper, removing a fistful of "acky," and smearing it all over his face and mouth and the closest piece of furniture. Thankfully, the habit was short-lived, and Ben clearly didn't remember it, but I did, in vivid sensory detail. I suspected it would be the kind of memory that would resurface in me from time to time as Ben grew older, especially when he was, like then, openly rebelling. But also, perhaps, when he got a college degree and a job and got married and became a know-it-all parent himself. I imagine all parents, including the father of that girl, carry with them such humbling images from when their offspring lived, blissfully, a little closer to the evolutionary tree.

I don't recall when I first learned about evolution, but I do remember being enthralled, like Spencer, by the idea of kinship with animals. I'm not talking about a sense of fascination and protectiveness, as with Woolly the caterpillar, or companionship, as with our cats. I'm talking about the search for complete identification with another creature that is alive, but also the container a kid can use to hold and carry around a newly born sense of self. Something similar to a spirit animal, I suppose. I'd tried out several candidates as a boy, my primary resource being the *Reader's Digest Fascinating World of Animals*—a massive, hardcover compendium of color photographs organized according to major ecosystems. When I was around Ben's age, I became enthralled by the photograph of a squirrel monkey: its small body, its big-eyed, friendly face, like a figurine in my mother's Kewpie doll collection. When I spotted a rubber replica of what appeared to be that same monkey in a dime store, I begged Mom until she got it for me. I named him Chico and spent hours with him in my bedroom, petting his rubber head and pretending to teach him to talk. One day, I safety-pinned him to my shoulder and wore him to school. The strong response from my classmates cured me of any remaining fascination with squirrel monkeys.

True spirit animals have little to do with such choices, however. They are gifted to you by the universe, or perhaps by a grandparent, which can be almost the same thing. Take me and tigers. Grandpa Andy had called me "Tiger" since I was a newborn, and throughout my childhood he and Grandma K bought me all kinds of tiger stuff: a tiger sleeping bag, a tiger pillow, plastic tiger toys, tiger pajamas and slippers. For a while, my bedroom was disguised as a jungle, the curtains and bedsheets printed with tigers and other wild animals—the largest indoor rain forest in the neighborhood. For my ninth birthday, Grandma commissioned Esther to paint a portrait of a tiger's face, which hung on my bedroom wall, surrounded by another half dozen tiger posters. They remained there until a different wildness infected me and were replaced by posters of Loni Anderson, Bo Derek, and Daisy Duke.

One thing I never took down was the tiger statue—a mighty ceramic Bengal, nearly a foot tall, perched on the edge of a rocky cliff, its fanged mouth open and roaring. That statue went everywhere with me, including my college dorm room and various apartments. It currently sat on my study bookshelf, where I could gaze at it between sentences. My grandparents gave it to me for Christmas 1973, when I was seven. Back then, I didn't think anything could be more ferocious, more beautiful, and that admiration carried over to real tigers. Not much later, I saw one up close for the first time. I don't remember where we were, maybe another zoo. After pushing my way through a crowd, I caught my first glimpse, which made my skin prickle. The tiger was bigger than I'd ever imagined, paws like pumpkins, a backside as broad as a diving board. It wasn't moving, yet its muscles twitched and shivered with a force close to electricity. I knew, however, that what was inside that tiger, what made it so powerful, could never run through a plug in my bedroom wall or be caged or contained by anything. The tiger was connected to a different source altogether.

As I grew older, I became less in tune with the transcendent energy of the tigers I saw and more aware of their cages. That is why I usually avoided visiting the Cat Complex at Henry Doorly Zoo, even though it had received national recognition for its husbandry of captive tigers, including a successful breeding program. The kids had become attached to several tiger cubs and liked to visit them with Steph, but I hadn't gone there in over a year.

Today was no different as I herded the boys and their cousins up the hill from Gorilla Valley and into the Desert Dome. As usual, the moment I stepped into that vast space, a sense of calm washed over me. The light filtering through the geodesic panels felt less punishing, the air drier, cleaner than what was outside or in the rain forest. Instead of the roar of waterfalls, there was the peaceful sound of water trickling against stone. The pathway was wide and clearly delineated against the sandy soil and rock walls. The spiky, interesting plants never shed their leaves or made messes. The creatures there, such as the kit fox, meerkats, and klipspringers, were smaller, their enclosures natural looking, with rocks and dirt and native plants. Everything was open to the vast domed space above, where the animals could see the sky and (I presumed) the stars.

In the Desert Dome, unlike the real desert, or even the Loess Hills just across the river, we did not have to worry something major would erode or disappear overnight or that one creature would hunt and kill another. That only happened inside the zoo's IMAX theater. Everything pretty much stayed the same in the dome, encouraging the illusion that nothing changed there or suffered or died.

After rounding a bend, we entered a Sonoran "canyon" that had always reminded me a little of Sabino. Below a cliff wall, there was a creek and a sandy flat where peccaries roamed as if they belonged there. Another carefree oasis. Then I looked up at the large cave along a rocky ledge. Behind thin wire mesh, there was a sleeping mountain lion, its back turned toward the tourists. I'd completely forgotten there was a lion on display here, and I wondered: Was this the cat named Omaha?

I hadn't thought about Omaha the cougar in quite some time. His story began in early October 2003, when several people reported seeing a mountain lion within Omaha city limits. A young male was eventually tracked and cornered in some bushes near the busiest intersection in town. A zoo official shot him with a tranquilizer dart, but when the big cat stumbled out of the brush, a frightened sheriff unloaded a twelve-gage into his leg. The injured, sedated lion was transported to Henry Doorly Zoo, where staff treated his wounds and Game and Parks officials deliberated his fate. They weren't sure where the cat originated, but he'd probably wandered here from out west, following hunting routes along the rivers. Some suggested he should be set free in the wilder panhandle of Nebraska, where resident populations of mountain lions had recently been reported, but game officials worried he would find his way back to the city. They looked into releasing him in another state, but there weren't any takers. It was finally determined that the best option was to keep him at the zoo. Someone wrote a letter to the newspaper suggesting they call him "Omaha," and the name stuck.

Mountain lions had been native to this part of the Midwest for centuries but were hunted off well before the turn of the century. Now, apparently, they were returning to the old home place. Confirmed sightings had increased during recent years but could still be counted on two hands. Omaha was one of the lucky ones, if you could call it that. The first documented sighting of a cougar in Iowa since 1867 was a roadkill specimen near Denison in 2001. Others had been shot and killed in the name of "public safety," even though attacks were incredibly rare and none had ever been reported in Nebraska or Iowa. Most of the reported sightings in our area had turned out to be raccoons, possums, dogs, and large house cats. So many false reports were made in Iowa that DNR officials had begun using the term "mountain lion hysteria."

The overreaction was perhaps understandable, given our natural history. Unlike Steph and others who'd grown up in bear country, the vast majority of Midwesterners were not accustomed to the presence of large predators. Along with the mountain lions, most resident populations of bears and wolves were extinguished in Iowa by the 1880s or earlier. Sasquatch, as far as I knew, had never set foot in the state.

So following the capture of Omaha, it was interesting (to say the least) to suddenly see articles and editorials in the local newspapers, as well as television reports, on the dangers of mountain lions and how to avoid being attacked by one. Children and small dogs were especially at risk, some said, and one concerned citizen claimed: "I don't let my dogs out by themselves, and I don't let my kids out by themselves." A local school canceled outdoor recesses when there was an unconfirmed sighting in the area. Other articles warned that lions prefer creek beds and places with dense tree growth, and to avoid encounters in those areas you should make a lot of noise, especially at dusk. For a while, the occasional sound of people banging pots and pans as they took out the garbage could be heard in our wooded neighborhood.

It seemed this cat had almost singlehandedly resurrected a latent fear of the predator in our local population, and maybe also a little respect and humility, though it was hard to tell sometimes. Omaha himself appeared indifferent to his celebrity status, as he continued to sleep with his back to the tourists. But was this actually Omaha? I couldn't tell for sure; the zoo had three other resident cougars, including a female they'd hoped might take a liking to him (had she?).

In a way it didn't matter. No matter where he was at the zoo, Omaha's story—the fact that he had a story, one that extended beyond the Cat Complex or the glass enclosure of the Dome— infected the place for me. Whatever illusion I had briefly entertained about a sanctuary free of unpleasant changes dissipated, leaving me with the now-familiar feelings of helplessness and guilt in the face of environmental degradation. Those feelings were intensified by the fact that, unlike the gorilla or the tiger or the vast majority of zoo residents, Omaha was one of our own, a native who was once wild and free, just like the nearby Loess Hills and Missouri River—just like most of America. Now, like them, he was permanently damaged, imprisoned by glass and concrete, dreaming away what remained of his pathetic life.

And there was nothing I or anyone could do to change that.

As I prepared to walk away, as usual, I added the Desert Dome to my mental list of places to be avoided during future zoo visits. Pretty soon, there'd be nothing left for me but the pygmy goats. I was falling in behind Steph and the kids, when I noticed the lion shift in his sleep, and his face became visible, resting on a foreleg. The effect on me was strange and held me in place. There was a familiarity in that face that went beyond the fact that I had seen other mountain lions and knew what they looked like. It was somehow like the face of the gorilla, a reflection of my own, or of some inner self that wasn't really the face of a primate at all but closer to those tigers in my childhood bedroom. The ones who used to stare at me from the posters, from the front of my pajama tops, from the pillow covers and curtains and the statue on the dresser.

Especially the statue. I could see that Bengal so clearly, perched nobly on his own cliff, not in my study in Council Bluffs but in my childhood bedroom, illuminated from below by the dim night-light. From the moment that figure entered my life when I was seven, it seemed to exert a gravitational force, especially the following Easter, after James. Lying in bed that night, I couldn't take my eyes off its face as I repeatedly prayed to God, demanding that he resurrect my brother, as he had his own son. I prayed until the silence seemed to warp into the face of the tiger, the countenance of a universe in which we and those we love are just another form of prey, as in those nature movies I hated, still hated—*You're on someone's menu the moment you hatch!*

But then that, too, changed. After, I don't know, a week, a month, a year of praying the same thing every night, the Tiger stopped being the silent response to the prayer, and became the prayer itself. The grief, the anger, the defiance in the face of a cosmic indifference that was or was not God—no one could tell me, for sure. I'd assumed I was alone with that prayer, those feelings, but then I realized I'd never been alone. The Tiger had been sending it up all along, on the edge of another cliff, frozen in its defining articulation—the roar—and doing so for me, for my family, for the world, twenty-four–seven.

That's what I saw in the face of the mountain lion, but also something else related to that old statue, but less about the face, the roar, than what I now remembered was written beneath the rock on which it stood: "To John Thomas Price. Christmas 1973. You're Grandpa's Tiger always." It was scripted by my grandmother's hand and, despite what the words said, there was no doubt who had given it to me and why. That tiger was not intended to be an expression of anger or defiance but of love. Her kind of love: ferocious, vigilant, self-sacrificing, enduring. Not the fearful, possessive, resentful love that is also born of suffering and had too often defined her. It was the former kind of love that had allowed her to survive the hardships and disappointments of her life, to care for sick family members, to follow her restless husband to Arizona, and then return home to Iowa, to live out her final years among family and the memory of family. To die on her own terms. It was the kind of love that had, as our trip to Lehigh confirmed, gone a long way toward filling the spaces left by loss.

How different, I wondered, was the mountain lion's story from my grandmother's? It might seem a stretch, but hadn't he, too, been guided back to the home of his ancestors by a fierce, instinctive love? One that in its own way had the power to heal what had once seemed beyond healing—in himself and in the land?

Their journeys had ended unexpectedly, as they all do, but that did not alter the power of their calling, which was this: to assist that love with my own. To offer up whatever meager gifts and abilities I possessed in service to the world around me—to become the prayer. For too long, when it came to the natural world, or my family and community, I had ceded that responsibility to other people and creatures, real and imaginary, who (with the sometimes help of my children) continued against my wishes to carry it back to me—the questions with wings. Sure, I had mourned losses in my life and in the life of the land, so much that it had paralyzed me at times. But that was no longer enough. It couldn't be enough. There was work to be done.

The nature of that work—like all true vocations—had very little to do with money, or with any unrealistic notions of success. In my case, its inspiration could be found in the daily responsibilities of being a parent, a caretaker, spilling over into my relationship to the natural world. It was the kind of caretaking demonstrated by those who'd saved this mountain lion from a place still unworthy of it. The kind demonstrated, as well, by the knowledgeable, dedicated people protecting and restoring the Loess Hills, the prairies, the rivers. People who, despite their own grief and anger, were working to make this a place worthy of the next mountain lion and the next—of all creatures, human and nonhuman, who wished to be at home here.

Although I didn't know it yet, I would, in my own ways, re-dedicate myself to joining that effort in the years ahead, and would look back on this moment with the mountain lion as an important step in that direction. It was a moment that never would have happened, however, without the original connection. And that had not been given to me by anything at the zoo or in a college science class or some informative field guide or death-obsessed nature program. Or anything in nature, really.

It had been given to me in my childhood, unintentionally, by my grandmother, in the form of a ceramic tiger. A piece of art. A symbol. The work of the writer I would become, had become, and needed to become again.

A few minutes later, standing in Hummingbird Canyon, I watched several of the tiny birds perched in the high branches and thought again of that time with my grandmother in Sabino when I was fourteen. We'd taken the shuttle to the far end of the canyon, where we got out to admire the view. Grandma's "bladder issues" necessitated that she return on the next ride, but she encouraged me to walk back on my own and do a little exploring. She promised to meet me somewhere along the way and waved from the back of the departing shuttle.

It was the first time I'd been alone during our stay in Arizona, maybe even longer, and I became almost giddy with freedom. The first thing I did was climb a nearby switchback trail for an even grander view of the canyon, taking in the jagged edge of the Acropolis Wall and the cactus-covered slopes and the creek, which was only a glinting, silver worm from that height. I took my time during the three-mile trek back down, stopping to admire a curiously twisted prickly pear or the yellow bloom of a desert marigold or to sit on one of the black-striped rocks and put my bare feet in the stream. Occasionally, there'd be an old stone staircase leading up to another viewpoint—I took all of them. For those couple of hours, I was no longer the self-conscious, isolated teenager. I had shed that skin, like one of the snakes I could swear I heard moving through the dry grass, becoming someone new. Someone who belonged.

Grandma met me at a small picnic area near the head of Sabino Dam trail. She must have been waiting the entire time, and I apologized, but she didn't scold me. She'd enjoyed sitting there, she said, in such a beautiful place. Together, we followed the creekside trail, which was more difficult than anticipated. It was narrow and rocky and pushed right up against another cliff wall. When I looked up, the ridgetops appeared at times to be leaning forward, threatening to topple. This is when I became a little dizzy, and Grandma pointed out the shady picnic bench near the willows.

We didn't see the hummingbirds right away; we heard them, that distinctive buzzing that resonates in the chest. Then one of them darted in front of us, then another, and then we saw them everywhere, perched on branches or levitating in front of the feeders, their iridescent little bodies changing colors when they entered the streams of light. I lost myself in their flight.

Back at Hummingbird Canyon, the birds weren't flying; they were resting on the branches, tiny and still, and it was Omaha and I was a forty-year-old man. But somehow the moment felt the same, which was different from the earlier moment with the mountain lion. That moment had been about desire and doing, about responsible action, which is essential. It seems to me now, though, that none of that is possible without this other kind of moment, when the monkey noise of the mind is silenced, and a person is liberated from all expectation. As I had been in Sabino— as perhaps she had been too. In my memory of that place, that moment, I am no longer the awkward teenager, and she is no longer the aging caretaker. No longer grandson and grandmother. Together, we are free from the desire to be perfect, to never fail or let our loved ones down. Free, even from the need to give or receive love. We just *are*. Like those tiny birds who were traversing the short space from one branch to another with as much thoughtless beauty as they had the two-thousand-mile journey, the lifetime, that had brought them there.

I could almost feel my grandmother's presence, hear the sound of those wings, that buzzing in the chest, and then I realized I was hearing it, somewhere in Hummingbird Canyon. I searched the grottos and couldn't spot any of them in flight, but the sound—can it be described as a sound?—persisted. I searched some more, until I heard the voices of my children. They were calling my name, and soon they marched around the rocky bend and took my hands. I wanted to stay where I was, but they were pulling me toward the next exhibit, the Kingdoms of the Night, and then back home, where the phone message from my father would be waiting. And then beyond, into the future.

The place they knew I needed to be, because . . . well . . . that's where they were.

15

The Witness Tree

THE ENDING WAS as she'd hoped it would be, I think. On the morning of Thursday, June 29, Mom visited Grandma at Friendship Haven and they had what she called a "very loving conversation." Later that afternoon, while we were at the zoo, she fed Niña a little broasted chicken and decided to take a nap. The nurse administered her eyedrops, she lay back on her pillow, and was gone.

When I first heard the news, I experienced a myriad of emotions, but the overwhelming feeling was of peace. That was partly the result of what I'd just experienced in Hummingbird Canyon, the sense of her presence, but I also felt that between her and me there was nothing left incomplete, that we had said and done all that needed to be said and done. I worried that wasn't the case for the boys, who had only really begun to know and love her. It would hit them very hard, I thought. When I first broke the news, they were with their cousins, and it didn't seem to register. Later that evening, in the middle of watching television, Ben burst into tears and crawled into my lap. Spencer stopped playing LEGOs for a moment to watch him, then returned to building his castle. We asked Spencer if he wanted to share his feelings, but he shook his head. After a few more minutes of listening to Ben cry, he got up and went to the kitchen.

The funeral was held July 3 at First Congregational Church. The pews were packed with generations of family, friends, and acquaintances. Grandma's mahogany urn was placed on the altar, in front of an illuminated stained-glass window, surrounded by flowers. The service was predominantly music and scripture readings, as she'd requested. As we sang the final hymn, I looked over at the boys. Spencer was still dry-eyed, his head snuggled into Stephanie's arm. Ben had apparently run out of tears the day before, but not questions, which he'd been asking throughout the service. Especially about cremation and how Gramma K could fit into such a small container.

"Is her face at the bottom or top of the jar, Dad?"

At the reception, while the boys and their cousins played in the toy room, we ate sandwiches in the fellowship hall and offered people a chance to stand up and share their memories. Mom had written a lovely tribute, and provided copies for everyone in attendance. I knew some of the stories and details she wrote about, including how Grandma cared for so many of her family members and how much she loved her grandchildren and great-grandchildren. Her relationship to Niña received a full paragraph, which was only proper. Some of the details were new to me, however, such as Grandma being the leader of my mom's Brownie and Girl Scout troops for fifteen years. Despite her dislike of camping (yet another characteristic we shared), she'd become a "master of building campfires, tying knots, and first aid," and entertained hundreds of children with her stories about the Brownie elves living in the woods and prairies they explored together. I wished my kids and I could have heard a few of those.

Then there were all the small acts of compassion my mother had observed while growing up. The two shivering, barefoot children who stood on their doorstep one Halloween, to whom my grandmother gave shoes and coats as well as trick-or-treat candy. The ten dollar bill she and Grandpa anonymously slipped into an elderly neighbor's mailbox, which was enough to feed her for a week. Grandma shoveling the driveway of another ailing neighbor and bringing in his mail as well as meals. The many car rides they gave to those without transportation, including children needing a lift to Sunday school and the woman with cerebral palsy who needed a lift everywhere. During the Depression, Grandma regularly fed the "hobos" who rode the rails and found their way to her door, her name being well known locally among those who shared poverty.

Several others stood up and offered similar stories about my grandmother's generosity and friendship. One woman described how when she was a little girl and her parents were struggling to support their family, Kathryn and Andy left bags of groceries and garden vegetables on their doorstep. I wondered if those vegetables had been harvested from her grandfather's garden in Otho? Her story and others, including my mother's, dismantled the myth that children aren't paying attention to the acts of kindness occurring in the adult world around them. That it is only our mistakes that matter to them.

When my turn came to share a memory, I struggled. As I walked to the microphone, my thoughts finally settled on a story that captured an aspect of my grandmother too often underappreciated, even by me. In high school, during another family trip to Arizona, Grandma decided to invite her neighbors over for dinner with us and thought it would be fun to make some margaritas. This was a special occasion—she rarely drank—and not just any tequila would do. She'd been told the best was to be found in Mexico, so she and I hopped into their giant white Lincoln and headed for the border. In Nogales, after she made her purchase, my attention was drawn to a large switchblade on display in a neighboring shop. I had a knife collection, I told her, and this was the missing piece. Within a minute the clerk was wrapping it up for me. Only after we'd left the shop did I sheepishly inform her it was against U.S. law to buy or sell that kind of knife or transport it into the country. She didn't seem worried. My resolve threatened to crumble, however, as we approached customs and I confronted the fact that we were about to attempt to smuggle both booze and an illegal weapon across the border.

"Calm down or you'll give us away," she scolded when she noticed how nervous I was. "I've put the stuff in my handbag, and unless you muck it up, they'll think I'm just a little old lady with a big white purse visiting Mexico with her grandson."

And that's exactly how it went down, I told everyone at the funeral. They laughed, which I thought Grandma would have appreciated. Then I felt the grief coming on, and my throat locked up. There was an awkward pause.

"In looking back over her last few months," I finally said, "I think my grandmother taught us all something about how to live and die with dignity."

Then I sat down.

I spent the Fourth of July cleaning out Grandma's apartment. The others in my family were enjoying the fireworks display from the grounds of the nearby Fort Museum, a replica of the original frontier outpost for which my hometown is named. Among other curiosities, it was well known for housing a replica of the Cardiff Giant. In 1868, a con man bought a five-ton chunk of Fort Dodge gypsum, had it carved into the shape of a colossal man, and buried it on a farm in New York state. It was then "accidentally" discovered and offered to the public as proof that giants once walked the earth, as it says in the sixth chapter of Genesis. Until the hoax was exposed, the giant claimed national headlines, fooling well-respected scientists and even Ralph Waldo Emerson, who declared that "it is undoubtedly a bona fide, petrified human being." My sisters and I visited the replica as kids whenever we went to the

Fort Museum with our grandparents. Grandmas K never let us linger there too long, however, because as my sisters' giggles inevitably reminded her, the giant was anatomically correct in all the wrong ways.

It would have been fun to visit the fort again, but I didn't really like fireworks shows—the noise, the sulfur smell, the crowds. Plus, for reasons I didn't share with my family, it wasn't my favorite holiday, especially during wartime. From the Vietnam War to the Cold War to the Iraq War, there had never seemed a time in my life when the country wasn't engaged in some kind of questionable conflict. I didn't begrudge anyone a little fun and sparklers, especially the kids, but for me the holiday seemed to call for a more reflective response. Or at least a more helpful one.

Helpful was what I hoped to be that particular evening. I knew it would be difficult for Mom to get started cleaning the apartment, and perhaps I could move things along a little. I placed one of Grandma's favorite albums on the player, and the Longines Symphonette (whoever they were) launched into a high-flying version of "Some Enchanted Evening." Then I began removing items from her drawers and shelves, folding the clothes in her closet and placing them in various boxes. It was an odd feeling. These were the artifacts of my grandmother's daily life, soon to be dispersed among individuals and families, some of them strangers, never to be assembled in one place again. I encountered several items that held personal stories and memories, like the porcelain roadrunner I'd always admired in their Arizona home. Many others reached beyond the boundaries of our relationship. Some were very old—a bent ring, a pressed flower—with no apparent monetary value but which undoubtedly had stories attached to them. Stories that were now gone.

After packing a few more boxes, I sat down on the couch and caught the scent of Ivory soap, her scent. I picked up my grandmother's diary, which I'd brought with me from Council Bluffs. As promised, this would be the first time I opened it. I removed the key from under the tape and unlocked the clasp. It was a multiyear diary, from 1930 to 1932, intended, as the cover page proclaimed, "for Recording Events Most Worthy of Remembering." The entries I read were scripted in blue and black ink by a teenager chronicling her adventures and friendships and crushes and dreams for the future, including her growing love for the young man who would become my grandfather. There was no mention of family hardship or disappointment, not even the Depression. She seemed to have been too busy having fun. Ice-skating on the Des Moines River or, in the summer, swimming in lakes; driving fast cars along country roads and all-night partying with her friends; dates with various beaus that—as she'd warned me—sometimes involved a little "necking." I didn't uncover any scandalous secrets, but on July 23, 1932, at the age of eighteen, she was arrested at a speakeasy with my grandfather. Although she claimed not to have touched a drop of illegal alcohol, she was hauled down to the police station with the rest of them and her name put "on the register." Her description of having to break the news to her mother made me laugh out loud.

"Was she ever angry," she reported. "Now I suppose I'll hear about that forever."

Passionate, adventurous, fun-loving, opinionated—she was right, this wasn't a Kathryn I had known. But it wasn't someone I didn't recognize or remember.

I put the diary aside, went over to the window, and looked out on the darkened courtyard. I could count maybe fifty lightning bugs outside, sparkling in the dark of the courtyard, in between bright flashes of fireworks. Like every other Iowa kid, including my grandmother, I used to catch fireflies by the dozens. Sometimes I'd put them in a pickle jar, place them on my bed stand, and try to read by their light. The next morning I'd always let them go. Like the frogs, these insects might be moving toward extinction, thanks to lawn chemicals and light pollution, which messes with their mating rituals. If that happens, the nighttime world will certainly be diminished, especially for children.

Grandma was beyond all that now, but the earthly challenges

remained for the rest of us. Including the challenge to remember. Perhaps that, too, was an antidote to despair and complacency. Whether the memories of a world still lit by fireflies, or of the wisdom gleaned from the life and death of a grandmother, I knew what had been before, and what could be again and why it mattered. That knowledge might serve as a lighted path through the darkness.

But what about my children? What memory of their great-grandmother's life—or my life or any life—would remain to help them through?

The next morning, Ben and Spencer and their cousins played in the front yard of my childhood home while my parents and the rest of us watched. A few of them, including Ben, asked Grandpa Tom to lift them into the big maple. Spencer and my sister Allyson's diapered boy, Owen, sat among the thick, exposed roots, talking and digging their hands into the dirt. Grandma was right; I couldn't imagine the world without my youngest sister and her family. When she was Spencer's age, I had played with her beneath the branches of that same maple. As a boy, I'd considered that tree my personal refuge, a ready-made fort where I often retreated for privacy or extended meditation or simply to achieve a larger view of the world. I knew every inch of it: the winding staircase of its branches, the various resting spots and their advantages, the mysterious, faded initials—"JB"—carved into one of the upper branches. *Who was this JB? A boy like me? Someone from another century, now dead and buried?* I'd had plenty of time to wonder, especially on my ninth birthday, when I got stuck on that same branch and had to be rescued by the fire department.

I wasn't alone in being drawn to that maple. For years it served as a kind of witness tree, the site of countless gatherings where neighborhood children held private confabs or plotted adventures or simply sought escape from the adult world. I recalled one such gathering on August 9, 1974, the evening President Nixon resigned. I'd recently turned eight, and an hour before his speech, I knew something major was happening. I'd known it the moment my mother reached into the cupboard, brought down the cans of Jolly Green Giant, and began to make five-can casserole. I was, by then, practiced at reading the tilt of the world by the kind of dinner my mother was serving. I knew that Crock-Pot turkey with stuffing meant it was a holiday or that Mom was pregnant. Pork cutlets, skillet-fried with pepper gravy and instant potatoes were meant to speak, with more or less success, to one of my father's moods. Creamed beef on toast was neutral, a yawner. Five-can casserole, however, was reserved for the worst in our lives, like in April, just after James. So when I saw my mother slam those cans, one by one, up into the snaggletooth of the electric opener where they dangled and jerked until the jagged tops of their skulls popped off, it felt like the room got smaller.

I joined Carrie Anne and Susan at the kitchen counter, climbing onto one of the soda fountain chairs. We peered down into the family room, at our father stretched out in the plush swivel chair staring at the television set. He was thirty-seven. Mom spooned casserole into our bowls and then set up TV trays for her and Dad. When President Nixon's face appeared, my parents put down their spoons and stared space-eyed at the screen. The president looked tired, like every other grown-up during that time, and talked in a language even I could understand about not being a quitter and about healing and "God Bless America."

"Is President Nixon quitting?" I asked.

"Yes," my mother replied.

I would've asked her why, but I already knew it was my fault. I'd often heard grown-ups say Nixon was a bad president, that he'd lied, and so I'd come to believe it and wished him to go away, just like I'd wished a lot of the problems of the time to go away. Problems that, despite our parents' best efforts, leaked into our lives through their casual conversations and the television news. I'd often heard Walter Cronkite refer to the Vietnam War, but I'd never asked my parents about it or anything else during that half hour. The evening news brought down an iron lid of silence on our home. During dinner, the TV was often out of sight but still blaring. Sometimes in the middle of eating, Dad would push back his chair from the table, stand, and stare down at the images on the screen—usually rough, shaky shadows of people tearing through jungles or city streets, carrying guns or signs or babies. People always seemed to be running then, the camera never still. Dad would sit back down and stare into his food, as if he'd been shushed.

The worried silence of my parents contrasted sharply with the approach of my childhood friends. My buddies and I had always talked openly about the problems of the world, about what our parents and other grown-ups were saying about the president and taxes (whatever they were) and the war and those they knew who'd died in the war and a lot of other things they didn't know we were paying attention to. We talked about what should be done about these problems—and something must be done, that much was certain. Like most children, we had yet to appreciate the gap between aspiration and reality, which is to say we had not yet relinquished courage and hope.

How exactly we should act on those convictions was another question altogether. Luckily, we had among us boys whose older siblings had been involved in a number of public protests and were more than happy to offer advice. Their suggestions included making protest signs, returning our plastic army men to the store, and drawing up draft cards and burning them—all of which we'd tried with few, if any, tangible results.

The purpose of streaking was even less clear to me. A friend explained that his college-age brother and his buddies had done it a lot to protest the war and had even gotten their names in the paper. I wasn't sure any cause was worth that kind of sacrifice. Besides, how would anyone know what you were protesting? It wasn't like you were wearing signs. I was assured people *would* know. That *lots* of people streak and *everybody* knows what it means. When a few of us actually tried it out, this did not seem to be the case. As we ran naked down busy Tenth Avenue, cars honked and passengers jerked their heads over their shoulders.

High-school football players, practicing on the stadium field, hooted and hollered as we ran by. During the final stretch toward home, a couple of dogs gave chase, barking and causing enough racket to bring several familiar mothers to their front doors. The looks on their faces did not suggest we were inspiring them to call their senators. What they did was call our mothers.

On the eve of President Nixon's resignation, however, it appeared my friends and their older siblings had been right: We had made a difference. We'd charged headfirst against the rules of society, against our own fears, and now the president, who all our parents had criticized, was quitting. It seemed safe to assume the end of the Vietnam War would quickly follow. But our parents did not seem to be in a celebratory mood. The way some of my friends had talked, getting rid of President Nixon would have everyone dancing in the streets and singing and tossing confetti. Maybe that was going on in their homes, but not mine. My parents seemed sad and sunken, as if the bones were crumbling inside them. Even my sisters sensed it. We lowered our spoons and made for the door.

From the front steps, we sized up the evening. The air was heavy and damp, as it always was in August, the sunlight dripping like honey from every surface. We headed for our preferred perch, the giant red maple, and it wasn't long before other kids started trickling in to sit with us in the grass beneath its branches. They'd been chased out of their homes, I assume, by the same silence that had chased us out of ours. Eventually, most of the kids in the neighborhood were there, beneath the tree, in the grass, sitting in the rough circle that was the custom of our tribe. Our kinship with one another was beyond question, forged as it had been by shared dreams, adventures, and tragedies. There was Dale, who'd lost his older brother to a respiratory disease. There was Mike, who would soon move to Missouri, where his parents would get divorced. There was my best friend, Andy, whose pilot father, in just a few days, would die in a crop-dusting accident. We all had or would have more than one reason to see what is missing in the world around us, and long to resurrect it.

Where that longing has taken them in the years since, only they could tell you, but I wonder sometimes if it didn't play a role in drawing me to the endangered prairies, to staying home and helping restore what had seemingly been lost. The "mistake" that had, as my grandmother put it, made all the difference.

Whatever the case, I think I can safely say that on the night President Nixon resigned we were not focused on what was missing in our lives, or in the world, but on what was already present. We had the tree, the grass, the twilight—that savannah-like meeting place of sun and shadow that still held the origins of not only our place but our species. And we had each other. There, in my front yard, beneath the maple, we talked and took in the last sweet breaths of summer, holding off any fears of the future. We remained there past dusk when the lights of the televisions could be seen all around, through the living room windows, flickering in sync. No one was calling to us. It was as if we'd been completely forgotten, which could be a beautiful thing as a kid.

We sat together a while longer on the cooling earth, until the fireflies came out in force and the cricket songs and the stars could be seen among the darkening branches. Then we pulled ourselves up and returned to the blue campfires that were our homes.

Now I was watching my own children, and the children of my sisters, play on that same tree after their first real experience of death. It was hard to predict how they would respond to this and future losses in their lives, or what we should do as parents to help them. Those responsibilities seemed to be getting more complex as the world got more complex, but that too was an illusion. I thought about all the disasters going on in the background of my grandmother's diary—the World War, the Dust Bowl, the Depression—and also something else from the tribute my mom had written:

"She loved being a mother, and I remember her telling me she would look into my crib and wonder if she'd done the right thing in the midst of the war to have brought a child into this world to face all the tragedies that were occurring. She later remarked that the world was still in a mess, but she knew she had made the right choice. She believed that those who were given life owed much to the world."

I suspected that part of what we owed the world was taking place right there, at the base of the tree and in its branches, though it was beyond adult control, as always. In the face of loss, our children had gone outside and found each other. I hoped that in the years to come they'd continue to rely on their friends and family, and on their own natural places, for reassurance and refuge. We owed them that possibility, at least—a freedom worth celebrating and defending. At the moment, it was their cousins and their own grandparents, and the gathering place was a maple tree, one that happened to connect their childhoods to mine, across the almost unimaginable border of a millennium.

Would they remember it? Would they remember anything from the last few months?

I watched them and took a deep breath, as I had back then, drawing into myself a little of what we had seen and done and might still do together as a family. All those future borders we would cross.

Then I released it.

Epilogue: Dust Motes, 2012

My family and I are walking along the ridge of Vincent Bluff, in the Loess Hills. The prairie is beginning to show off its summer colors a little early, thanks to an unusually warm spring. Black-eyed Susans, oxeye sunflowers, ironweed. The tall milkweeds have me anticipating the time in August and September when we'll start collecting monarch caterpillars to raise, tag, and release. We started doing this after learning that monarchs hatched in captivity have a higher survival rate than those in the wild. This generation of monarchs, known as the Methuselah generation, will migrate three thousand miles to the breeding grounds in the highlands of Central Mexico. In early November, around El Día de los Muertos, they will arrive at the same mountain forest of oyamel fir trees that they have for centuries. The local people in Michoacán believe the butterflies to be the souls of dead children, and the Aztecs considered them ancestral spirits. All of them returning home.

This week marks the sixth anniversary of my grandmother's death, and it feels like we, too, have traveled thousands of miles. As I walk behind Ben and Spencer, I can hardly believe how tall they are getting, too early, I think, like some of the prairie plants around us. Ben is almost twelve and will be attending middle school in the fall. On the cusp of adolescence, he is leading us once again into uncharted territory as parents. Spencer is nine and still leading us on excursions into nature, but is (thankfully) less likely to do so naked. His areas of expertise have branched beyond worms and woolly bears, though he still loves them, to include pandas, fancy rats, and rhinos. He is a dues-paying member of the World Wildlife Fund, and for his last couple of birthday parties he's requested that those attending donate to that organization. If they wanted to also give him a LEGO set, that was fine too.

The biggest change of all, however, is not very tall and is running out in front of Ben and Spencer. He is a blond, curly-haired two-year-old named Alden James Gale Price, born October 6, 2009. We decided to have another child in the fall of 2006, but delayed until Steph had an MRI and a few more "all clears" from her doctor. After all the careful deliberations, as well as our advanced age, you'd think the universe would have rewarded us with a mellow, easygoing child who likes to sleep, but that wasn't the case. He's been the wildest, most energetic of all our children, as if he knew how lucky he was to be born and decided to hit the ground running.

And running is what he's been doing during most of our time on Vincent Bluff, like on every other family excursion. His brothers are having major difficulty keeping up with him. Steph and I know we can't keep up. That's why the outdoors have become the best option for him, and us, where there are no cars to worry about, no concrete to fall on, no crowds of children to accidentally plow into. No apologies. He's gotten away from us a few times in public, but never very far—his mass of curly blond locks makes him easy to spot. I guess the universe did help us in that regard. He looks like a miniature Art Garfunkel.

The presence of Alden is a constant reminder of what I recognize as a seismic shift in my life perspective since the spring of 2006, which I'm still trying to fully understand. I didn't think such change was possible, in part because of my cynicism about the "conversion stories" of others. Which was only an excuse, of course, for not working for such a change in my own life—not opening myself up to the possibility of that change. Challenges remain, and I sometimes feel my heart "wrinkle" (as Spencer once put it) as I slip back into the old, unhealthy habits. But there have been no more cardiac "events," and I have, in general, lived my life with renewed conviction and care. Especially in my role as a father, spending more time with Steph and the boys, more time engaged with the beauty of the world around and within them.

Thanks to Ben and Spencer, some things have not changed. Though they are growing up and, as all the politicians are saying on TV, they "represent the future," the boys have become fierce defenders of tradition. International Ben and Spencer Days, for instance. Despite my initial resistance, those holidays have become welcome events in our family, held exactly six months after each of their birthdays. The festivities were small at first, a couple of presents and maybe breakfast in bed, then ballooned into small family vacations. Two years ago, for International Spencer Day, we traveled to Tennessee to see the Chinese pandas at the Memphis Zoo. Last year, on International Ben Day, we traveled to Minneapolis to see the King Tut exhibit and an actual mummy on display in their Science Museum—Ben's fascination with the macabre continues. It will be interesting to see where International Alden Day will take us. Given his early personality, we're hoping it doesn't involve jumping out of a plane.

For Ben and Spencer, nature remains the primary habitat, and it is an expanding one. Just last week, they attended two "nature camps" connected to family tradition. The first was sponsored by Hitchcock Nature Center, one of our favorite places in the Loess Hills, where they learned about local wildlife and the ecosystems that sustain them: the dry loess prairies, the burr oak savannahs, the mesic oak woodlands. Since 2006, we've spent many hours hiking together at Hitchcock, and Ben and Spencer have attended numerous camps there. I've also given readings and nature writing workshops at the lodge overlooking the hills and the Missouri River Valley—a nationally recognized spot for observing raptor migrations. Last year, we participated in a "prairie rescue day" at Hitchcock, where we helped remove invasive species from a hillside near the trail. There was some initial controversy when Spencer refused to help cut down red cedar trees, but the natural resource specialist, Chad Graeve, was nice enough to reassign him to the less traumatic "shrubbery patrol."

We have since walked that trail and others at Hitchcock, admiring the reinvigorated grasses and wildflowers, and in the hillsides, examining the occasional clumps of rocklike, compressed soil. These ancient concretions, each with their own unique shape, are traditionally called "Loess Kinder"—children of the dust—as if the soil beneath our feet is just another kind of family. One that has become part of our own.

The other nature camp the boys attended last week was "Camp Grandma and Grandpa." This was the first of several similar camps they'll be attending this summer, including a July trip to Idaho to visit Steph's folks. While there, they will attend the same church camp in the Sawtooth Mountains that their mother did as a girl, and there will be fishing. Last weekend, however, it was off to Fort Dodge. While Alden stayed home to keep us on our toes, Ben and Spencer spent a few days with my parents, swimming, visiting parks and a botanical garden, and playing in my childhood yard. Mom continues to miss Grandma K, but she and Dad are busy creating their own memories and traditions as grandparents, which has included encouraging a love of nature in all their grandkids.

Back in January, for instance, my parents purchased tickets for Spencer to meet his hero, Dr. Jane Goodall, in Des Moines. For this very special event Spencer brought along "Grindor," his stuffed rhinoceros buddy. Last year, when he was in second grade, a couple of kids teased him for carrying his toy panda on the school bus, which confirmed that not much had changed since I went to school with Chico the spider monkey pinned to my shoulder. For a while, Spencer quit carrying around "Pandy" and his other stuffed animals, which made us sadder than expected. Then he and I saw a documentary film on Jane Goodall during which she showed off her own stuffed animal toy, a banana-holding monkey named "Mr. H." He was given to her by a friend, Gary Haun, who'd lost his eyesight in the U.S. Marines and had, against great odds, become a successful magician. The gift lifted her spirits, reminding her of Gary's message: "Don't give up when something goes wrong in your life. Work hard and you can overcome most obstacles."

But Jane also said Mr. H reminded her of the toy chimpanzee her father had given her when she was a child. His name was "Jubilee," and she claimed he was the original inspiration for her love of chimps and for her future activism on their behalf. Jubilee remained in her London home, but she carried Mr. H everywhere . she traveled, as a kind of ambassador of hope.

Spencer was thrilled to see she'd brought Mr. H to her lecture in Des Moines. Afterward, he and Jane posed for a picture together, both holding their so-called imaginary friends.

And, of course, Baby is still with us. Whatever jealousy he felt when Spencer began hanging out mostly with his stuffed animal friends has been more than compensated by the attention he's getting from Alden. They've established their own vocabulary of love, which includes less rock throwing and more bed-jumping and full-body coloring. One afternoon, we discovered that Alden had used his new markers to color Baby's entire face—and his own—blue and green. For a while, they looked like two orbiting planets, which, we know from experience, is how Baby prefers it.

Alden is, in fact, carrying Baby with him right now as he runs across the Vincent Bluff prairie. Although it feels worlds away, Vincent Bluff is just a few blocks from where we live in Council Bluffs, thirty-seven acres of restored virgin Loess Hills prairie and woodlands. Its existence is a small miracle, surrounded on all sides by fast food restaurants, residential neighborhoods, and the interstate. The Loess Hills Preservation Society, made up of conservationists, private landowners, concerned citizens, and some corporate donors, worked hard to preserve this local treasure. They've also worked with city, county, state, and federal agencies to drastically reduce the destruction of the hills in our area for landfill and new development. This is the kind of cooperation I'd thought impossible just a few years before, mostly because I hadn't been paying attention to what I didn't want to see.

On May 16, 2009, Vincent Bluff became the first urban prairie in Iowa to be declared a state preserve. I was invited to give one of the dedication speeches by preserve manager Glenn Pollock, who'd read my first book, *Not Just Any Land*. My speech focused on what this wild place in the heart of our city would mean for our children:

> They and their friends and families will be able to enjoy the magnificent views and wander among the tall grasses, perhaps becoming lost in them a time or two. They will be able to help gather prairie seeds and plant them, and will encounter all kinds of amazing creatures who, like them, consider this place home.

What I didn't talk about was what the dedication of Vincent Bluff meant to me, as a writer and citizen of the hills. Composing that short dedication was part of a renewed effort to use my writing in service to the places I love, rather than as an escape from them. Following my grandmother's death, I set aside the novel and returned with fresh commitment to writing about family and the landscapes of home. I put those essays together with a number of others I'd written over the years, and discovered they were all linked by the theme of "kinship," which I defined in my journal as "the familial embrace of nature, body, and spirit." The discovery of this theme surprised me, because it seemed to embrace the very powerlessness I'd once feared. It also revealed what should have been obvious all along: We do not choose the places into which we are born, any more than we choose our families or our bodies. The choice is whether or not to return that embrace, and to live fully within in it—as you would, say, the embrace of a grandmother.

Perhaps inspired by Spencer's alter ego, that prolific and engaging writer known as Tony Johnson, I entitled the book *Man Killed by Pheasant and Other Kinships*, foregrounding the story of the pheasant that flew in the window of the Tercel, and the flooded summer that so transformed my attitude toward the Iowa landscape. The book itself helped transform what I saw as my primary role as a writer, from increasingly frustrated isolation to more community involvement. Since its publication in 2008, I've given readings and dedications at several local and national prairie events, including writing the script for a short film about the Loess Hills. Off the page, I've been spending a lot more time in those hills, alone and with Steph and the boys, where we still confront destruction and despair but also beauty and hope as we meet those who are successfully working to preserve, restore, and celebrate these fragile giants. We are more committed than ever to helping them.

Vincent Bluff represented all this for me, and more. After a season of questions about my life in this place, it had become a kind of answer. One that, like so many I'd been searching for, was right there in front of me all along.

But so many questions remain, as I'm reminded when we return to the house. Before going inside, we decide to hang out in the yard awhile to let Alden (and Baby) work off a little more pluck. Steph and I are hoping—praying—for an early bedtime. Alden charges down to the edge of the woods, where six years ago Spencer found that first spring worm, and he and his brothers begin turning over rocks. We're not close enough to see what they've found, but Alden's squeals suggest the earth there is just as feral as it's always been.

Steph and I are watching them from the stairs, near the "Fairy Garden"—the most recent addition to the No-Kill Zone. One of the reasons it was created was because Alden has turned out to be as fanatical about enforcing the No-Kill law as his brothers. Just this spring there was an incident between Alden and another boy over the fate of an anthill in the driveway. It ended with the other boy getting pushed to the ground. This was not acceptable, of course, and he had to come inside for the obligatory time-out, but it wasn't that surprising given his role models. Afterward, Alden came up with a brilliant strategy to avoid similar conflicts in the future: He began bringing the ants and any other bugs he could find indoors and letting them loose in the living room.

Our history with ants made this untenable, but we had a hard time coming up with alternatives. Spencer suggested resurrecting his International Woolly Bear Preserve, which we'd been forced to "set free" a few years ago, thanks to all the insects he and Ben kept putting in the terrarium. There were so many crawling around inside, it had begun to resemble a beehive. The same problem would no doubt occur with Alden, but then Steph suggested we simply move the Woolly Bear Preserve outside. There was a small flower garden near the house, where Ben and Spencer had already been relocating "endangered" insects—why not expand it and encourage Alden to do the same? We got out the shovels and the pitchforks, tore up more bluegrass, and replaced it with flowers and rocks and other natural artifacts the boys had collected over the years, such as fossils and lava pumice and animal bones—too many bones, probably.

"It looks like a murder happened here," Ben commented after we completed the work. "I *like* it."

Alden was allowed to christen the new space and, despite the bones, dubbed it the "Fairy Garden." This was likely due to the influence of Missy, who is William's little sister and Alden's frequent playmate. Her favorite movie is *Tinker Bell*, which she and Alden have watched several times together. Ben and Spencer cringed when they heard the name of the new refuge, but have since helped populate it with fairy figurines and gnome houses and even a solar-powered, glowing owl—or "Hoo-Hoo," as Alden calls his favorite bird. As the number of insects, flowers, and personal artifacts has grown, it has also become a refuge for stories and memories. It's almost like the boys are writing their own autobiographies, the purpose of which, as Anaïs Nin once said, is "to taste life twice, in the moment and in retrospect."

It is impossible for me not to see it that way as well, and the yard in general. The past lives all around me. As I watch the boys playing in the far corner, near the woods, I'm reminded how they used to peek around the bluff to see if the woodchuck had returned to her secret den, but I think they've finally given that up. The yard and woods have continued to attract wildlife—raccoons, rabbits, deer, owls, hawks, buzzards, possums, skunks, turkeys, and even a peacock, which brought some excitement to the neighborhood. We have yet to see a mountain lion, but one evening we watched a red fox trot through our yard. Unfortunately, we haven't seen any woodchucks for several years now, perhaps because of the foxes, or because there is no longer a garden in Neighbor Henry's yard. He passed away a few months after my grandmother. It was that kind of summer: Grandma K, Aunt Esther, Neighbor Henry, and then Mrs. Freeburg, the kindhearted woman who stayed with us the Easter weekend when James died. She'd long since moved to California, so the boys never met her, but she sent them each a handmade stuffed rabbit when they were babies. Just like she did when my sisters and I were in the crib. We keep the bunnies in their bedrooms, and even though they don't remember, I do.

There have been more losses, including both of our cats, Tigger and Dorothy. A new cat has joined us, Sofia, named after the wife of Tolstoy—another guy with a conversion story to tell. We erected a couple of stone markers in the backyard for the cats, which the boys used to visit regularly, just like they used to stand at the fence bordering Henry's yard and stare into the overgrown weed patch that was once his garden.

Now they just run on by.

Inside the house, we're trying to settle Alden down, but that's proving to be difficult. The living room floor is covered with distractions—toys and pieces of toys and markers and coloring books. Two chairs and several couch cushions have been upended, and Alden is using his plastic hammer to "play" the piano. It looks (and sounds) as if a bomb went off, which is yet another thing that hasn't changed. As for general maintenance, the house and I continue to have our occasional battles, including one the other day involving a plunger, a monkey wrench, and a lot of expletives. But I have increasingly come to believe that a house, as Willa Cather put it, "can never be beautiful until it has been lived in for a long time. An old house built and furnished in miserable taste is more beautiful than a new house built and furnished in correct taste. The beauty lies in the associations that cluster around it, the way in which the house has fitted itself to the people."

Which it certainly has, if this glorious mess is any indication. At the moment, Ben is steering clear of the rubble and the noise, sitting at the dining room table where he can better organize his Pokémon cards for the next exchange with William. Next to him on the table is the collapsible butterfly habitat, which in a little over a month will house the monarch caterpillars. It has been a temporary home to a number of different creatures, including hundreds of praying mantis babies that hatched out of a mail-order egg sac Ben got for Christmas—apparently Santa hadn't learned his lesson with the Triops. Actually, Ben only received the mantis order form at Christmas, on which the company promised not to send the egg sac until spring. It arrived in February and hatched during a snowstorm. We spent the remaining weeks of winter searching far and wide for fruit fly distributors and trying to keep the mini-mantids from killing each other off entirely. By the time we set the last dozen or so free in the yard that spring, Steph was walking around the house with them perched on her arms and shoulders, hand-feeding them pinhead crickets.

We'd come a long way since Heirodula.

Spencer, true to form, had not participated in the cricket sacrifices, but later he did enjoy collecting the empty egg sacs he found in the yard, as well as the many encounters he had with the grown-up mantids. A number of those egg sacs ended up in his egg-carton nature collection. That is yet another tradition both he and Ben have passed on to Alden, helping him decorate and fill his own carton with an assortment of feathers and cicada husks and discarded toenail clippings. He is especially interested in the seashells we keep in the crystal bowl on the piano, and a few minutes ago, Spencer was nice enough to spread them all out on the floor. Now he is helping his little brother organize them into different sizes and shapes, and using our seashell identification guide to determine what kinds of animals once lived in them.

The shells also contained memories. Some of them were collected on the Oregon coast in August 2006, right about the time Steph and I decided we both wanted another child. We were staying in Yachats, along with the rest of Steph's family, to celebrate her parents' fiftieth wedding anniversary. We were about to take another giant risk as parents, and the presence of the generations, the conversations and stories, the laughter, made the decision seem even more right. The boys were oblivious to whatever new territory we were about to enter as a family. The beach was just down from our hotel, and every morning they rushed out to play with their cousins in the sand and run along the edges of the waves. While exploring tidal pools, they discovered all kinds of creatures, dead and alive, too numerous and strange to be entirely contained by the imagination, and certainly not by an egg carton.

Every once in a while, we saw a California gray whale shoot spray out of the ocean, part of a residential pod that didn't migrate with the others. For those few whales, that relatively small, nondescript stretch of ocean satisfied their needs, so they stayed put. It was a choice I had in common with them, set against the much larger migrations of our kind, of time itself. "One shared it," Nabokov said about time, "just as excited bathers share shining seawater—with creatures that were not oneself, but were joined to one by time's common flow, an environment quite different from the spatial world, which not only man but apes and butterflies can perceive."

Learning to live and love completely, at home within that flow, was the gift of that short stretch in my life. I can appreciate that now. But the mystery of time remains, the questions unanswered about what endures and what is lost.

It is now midevening and the descending sun is shining directly in the windows, illuminating a million dust motes, so that the beams seem to take on substance, perhaps like the Sun Bridge the Ioway believed appears from time to time in these hills. Alden is buck-naked and playing a game where he puts two or three seashells on his head and marches around, clucking like a chicken. Spencer is laughing hysterically, as am I, which just amplifies the craziness. Suddenly, Alden enters one of the sunbeams and stops. He reaches out his hand, grabs at the air, and kisses his fist.

"Gamma K!" he exclaims, then goes back to marching and clucking.

I am shocked, but then I remember.

"Did you teach him that, Spencer?" I ask.

He smiles and nods, shyly.

In the fall after Grandma died, Spencer still hadn't talked much about his feelings, although the nightmares had pretty much stopped. I didn't want to force things and risk sending him back to that dark place or worse. Then, one evening, he and I were snuggling on the living room couch, discussing the monarch butterflies we'd raised from caterpillars. We'd released them a few weeks earlier, the beginning of their long journey to that forest in Mexico where the people would welcome them home as kin. The descendants of those butterflies hopefully would return the next summer to lay eggs on the same honeyvine in our yard, which somehow they remembered, and the cycle would begin again.

We were talking about all that when Spencer grabbed at the air and kissed his fist, nearly knocking my glasses off. I asked him what was up.

"I'm kissing Gramma K," he replied. "In the dust fairies."

I knew he was referring to the dust motes sparkling in the sunbeams coming through the window, but I didn't get the Gramma K part. He must have seen the confusion on my face.

"You know, like what Gramma K and the minister said," he added, matter-of-factly.

That sounded a bit spooky. I asked him what he meant, and though it took me a while to translate, I thought I finally understood. When Spencer talked with Grandma K on the phone, back when he was having all those nightmares, he asked her why she had to die and if he would ever see her again. He said she promised him he *would* see her again and that she would *always* watch over him. That she would never, ever leave him. Then, at her memorial service, the minister talked about the dust (ashes to ashes, etc.), and Spencer put two and two together.

"I see her in the dust fairies and everywhere," he told me on the couch. "So I'm not sad."

The two promises, hers and the minister's, along with the promises of the natural world, had become entwined in his mind, answering the great mystery: She had returned to dust and, because of love, had returned to us. To stay.

It was over so quickly, that sweet assurance, but now, six years later, it has come back around. Passing from Spencer to his little brother. And then to me, the father with all the questions.

As if on wings.

Acknowledgments

It is never easy to have a memoirist in the family, especially one whose primary subject *is* their family. So, first and foremost, I want to thank my family for their ongoing love and support, especially my heroic wife, Stephanie, and our three wonderful sons: Ben, Spencer, and Alden. You have enriched my life beyond measure. Also, my parents, Tom and Sondra Price, and my sisters, Carrie Anne, Susan, and Allyson, and their families, including brothers-in-law Mark Whittaker and Jason Rushford, and all my nieces and nephews: Ian, Abby, Grace, Anna, Owen, Seth, and Luke. Love and thanks, as well, to my Idaho family, including Gary and Helen Strine, Cindy and Bill McDonald, Becky and Joe Parkinson, Amy and Scott Truksa, and their great kids: Kate, Gary, Luke, Tyler, Cole, and Christopher.

Eternal gratitude goes out to my agent, Joanne Wyckoff at Carol Mann Agency, for her vision and tireless effort on behalf of this story. Working with Shambhala Publications has long been a dream of mine, and I want to thank everyone there, especially my gifted and magnanimous editor, Jennifer Urban-Brown. A number of good friends offered me wisdom and encouragement while completing this book. These include: Julene Bair, Chip Blake, Tracy Bridgeford, Holly Carver, Chris Cokinos, Diane Horton Comer, Elizabeth Dodd, Hope Edelman, Tom Montgomery Fate, Kristin Girten, Jen Henderson, Patricia Henley, Merloyd Lawrence, Kathe Lison, Elmar Lueth, Sue Maher, John and Barb McKenna, Kate Miles, Michele Morano, Dave Pantos, Joe Price, Andy Nesler, Ladette Randolph, Jennifer Sahn, Steve Semken, Ned Stuckey-French, and Mary Swander. Thanks, as well, to Maria Knudtsen for all the zoo facts, to Deborah Lewis for her help with the flora and fauna of Dolliver State Park, and to Chad Graeve, Terry Oswald, Glenn Pollack, and the Loess Hills Preservation Society for providing me with essential information about the Loess Hills—I hope this book, in some small way, gives back to the "fragile giants" we love. We are blessed with wonderful neighbors, who have opened their hearts and, equally important, their yards to our children: the Evezic family, Bob and Elaine Jacobsen, Steve and Nancy Mether, and the Silik family. I am deeply indebted to the Sturm family for allowing their beautiful Loess Hills property to become a second home for our children.

The Black Earth Institute helped me think through many of the ideas informing this book, and provided an engaging community in which to explore and celebrate the intertwining of nature, spirituality, and social justice. I'm deeply grateful for the support of my colleagues, friends, and students at the University of Nebraska at Omaha, particularly my creative nonfiction colleagues: Molly Garriott, Jody Keisner, Tammie Kennedy, Lisa Knopp, Elizabeth Mack, and John McKenna. Susan Maher and Bob Darcy, as chairs of the English Department, and Dave Boocker, Dean of the College of Arts and Sciences, provided essential assistance. Completing this book would not have been possible without the generosity of the Kinney Family Foundation—thank you Yvette and Doug for all you're doing to support creative nonfiction writing at UNO!

Cheers to Kate Miles and everyone at the awesome *Hawk & Handsaw: The Journal of Creative Sustainability,* which published an earlier version of "Not So Golden Nuggets." Portions of "The Witness Tree" were included in talks I gave sponsored by Iowa Humanities and Trees Forever, and reprinted in *Voices from the Prairie*—thank you to those who made that writing possible.

Finally, I want to dedicate this book to two people who never met each other but who are the inspiration behind every word: my grandmother Kathryn Anderson and our youngest son, Alden James Gale Price. Thank you for awakening me, anew, to the beautiful adventure of life.

About the Author

MIKE WHYE

JOHN T. PRICE is the author of the memoir *Man Killed by Pheasant and Other Kinships* and *Not Just Any Land* and is a recipient of an NEA fellowship. His work has appeared in numerous journals, magazines, and anthologies, including *Orion, Best Spiritual Writing,* and *In Brief: Short Takes on the Personal*. He lives with his family in western Iowa and teaches at the University of Nebraska at Omaha.